# Gender Capital at Work

# Gender Capital at Work

## Intersections of Femininity, Masculinity, Class and Occupation

Kate Huppatz
*University of Western Sydney, Australia*

First published 2012 by
PALGRAVE MACMILLAN

Palgrave Macmillan in the UK is an imprint of Macmillan Publishers Limited, registered in England, company number 785998, of Houndmills, Basingstoke, Hampshire RG21 6XS.

Palgrave Macmillan in the US is a division of St Martin's Press LLC, 175 Fifth Avenue, New York, NY 10010.

Palgrave Macmillan is the global academic imprint of the above companies and has companies and representatives throughout the world.

Palgrave® and Macmillan® are registered trademarks in the United States, the United Kingdom, Europe and other countries.

ISBN 978–0–230–25199–1

This book is printed on paper suitable for recycling and made from fully managed and sustained forest sources. Logging, pulping and manufacturing processes are expected to conform to the environmental regulations of the country of origin.

A catalogue record for this book is available from the British Library.

A catalog record for this book is available from the Library of Congress.

10   9   8   7   6   5   4   3   2   1
21  20  19  18  17  16  15  14  13  12

Printed and bound in Great Britain by
CPI Antony Rowe, Chippenham and Eastbourne

*For my beautiful daughters: Ava and Audrey*

# Contents

# Acknowledgements

I am incredibly grateful to the workers who shared their time and personal experiences with me. I also wish to thank Susan Goodwin for her supervision of the thesis from which this book originated and for her feedback on earlier versions of the nursing and theory chapters. Finally, I wish to give special thanks to my husband for his love and support throughout the process of writing this book.

# Part I
# Gender, Class, Work and Reworking Bourdieu

# 1
# Introduction

In recent history workforces in rich, industrialised nations have been subject to a number of transformations. One of the largest changes is that women have entered the paid labour market in large numbers so that they now make up almost 50 per cent of the workforces in the UK and Australia (ABS, 2011; McDowell, 2009). However, occupations are horizontally segregated so that women continue to be clustered in certain occupational spaces and retain distance from others. For example, women congregate in occupations like nursing, teaching, social work, retail work, child care, beauty work and hairdressing but largely do not participate in carpentry, engineering, policing, mining and information technology. At the same time, men tend to be positioned in the occupational spaces that women are mostly absent from and appear to be largely quarantined from feminised work. Furthermore, some of these feminised and masculinised jobs are becoming *more* gendered (for example, in the UK and Australia the proportion of social workers who are female have increased since the 1990s (Meagher and Healy, 2005: 42; Perry and Cree, 2003; 376)) despite the introduction of equal opportunity policies and the weakening of gender norms in many areas of public life.

This perpetuation of gender segregation is problematical because 'women's work' tends to be treated as unequal to 'men's work'. In particular, masculinised occupations tend to be issued with more status and more pay than feminised occupations. In addition, occupational segregation results in women and men being limited to certain activities and therefore our economies are not necessarily making the best use of the population's abilities, and this potentially results in a loss of recruits for employers as well as skills shortages (The Trade and Industry Committee, 2005). Furthermore, the different values placed on men's and women's labour mean that an inequality exists within feminised jobs – they are vertically segregated within so that when men do enter feminised work, they appear to dominate the top positions.

Another significant and related change in the labour markets in countries like the UK and Australia is that the service economy has grown. Many commentators (see, for example, McDowell, 2009) have argued that because manufacturing work has declined and because women have progressively moved into the labour force, work that was previously carried out in the home is now carried out in the public realm and this labour constitutes a service economy. Service work typically involves caring for the bodily needs of others and a social relationship with customers (see McDowell, 2009) and often requires a kind of emotional labour as well as a certain bodily labour and so is 'embodied work' (McDowell, 2009). Moreover, it is feminised in that it is largely women who carry out this labour (all of the feminised jobs listed above may be loosely defined as service jobs), considered less respectable than rational and knowledge-creating work and it is mostly poorly paid.

These changes in the labour market have implications for the gender and class identities and practices of workers and they suggest that certain occupations and types of labour are gendered and classed. This means that workforce patterns have implications for the production and reproduction of gender and class, and this book aims to argue that a *gender economy* exists so that gendered embodiments are forms of wealth that operate as assets in the labour market.

## Motivations

However, this gender economy is difficult to grasp with many of the conceptual tools that are currently available in sociological theory. In particular, many theoretical approaches cannot grasp the intersections of gender and class in workers' occupational choices and pathways. Both my mother's work story, as well as my own work story, illustrate the need for a more complex theoretical approach. My mother grew up in a poor farming community in an era in which gender roles were particularly rigid and nursing or secretarial work were presented as her *only* choices. Neither of these options were very appealing to my mother (she would have preferred to be a doctor or a vet) but she 'chose' nursing because women were paid to carry out hospital-based training at the time and so it best suited her family's economic position and because nursing involves anatomical knowledge and so is most similar to her real preferences. This work story suggests that my mother's gendered work pathway was initiated by force, albeit a gentle kind – her choice was the result of her gendered and classed circumstances. My story is a little different. Unlike my mother, I had a number of choices available when I initially entered the workforce. However, I originally chose a career that is also feminised – a social work career. I made this decision for reasons unknown to me at the time, except that I thought I should be involved in 'caring' of some sort. Here, when I reflect back, an unconscious 'gender agenda' was at work, as well as perhaps class aspiration (and this was a more respectable choice than glamour modelling – an occupation that one of my secondary teachers suggested I was most suitable for). Thus, both my gender and class histories, positions and identities informed my decision.

When I sought to make sense of our experiences I realised that gender segregation is an issue that requires a more complex approach than what role theory, socio-biological theory or an understanding of gender discrimination can provide. It requires an understanding of how both choice *and* force operate in career pathways and also an understanding of how both gender *and* class processes impact career choices and trajectories. This book attempts to provide such an approach. Through an examination of the operation of 'gender capital' this book argues that a Bourdieusian approach with a focus on social practice provides a more sophisticated understanding of the processes that produce and reproduce gendered and classed work as well as workers.

## Aims

As the discussion above indicates, in exploring the gender economy this book aims to achieve several ambitions at once. First, this book hopes to shed further light on why certain jobs are produced and reproduced as feminine; it intends to understand why women and men continue to be segregated in their labour activities, identities and positions. Second, this book aims to explore how masculinity and femininity, maleness and femaleness are traded on in the labour market; I am attempting to build on the work of Bourdieusian feminists that have theorised before me (see for example, McCall (1992), Skeggs (1997) and Lovell (2000)) and to make a case for the usefulness of the concept 'gender capital'. Third, this book hopes to build on previous literature concerning aesthetic labour and emotional work in order to indicate its role in the gender economy. This is achieved through the examination of the operation of gender capital in four feminised occupations that may be broadly defined as service jobs: nursing, social work, exotic dancing and hairdressing.

Finally, all four of these occupations contain hierarchies in terms of positions as well as workplaces. They are also allocated varying amounts of respectability and are associated with different class cultures. This means that opportunities to enter and succeed in these occupations appear to be enabled or constrained by both class and gender. Therefore, my fourth aim is to explore the class processes in these occupations and their relationship with gender; how class and gender intersect in these occupations. In doing so, I hope to depict the feminisation of these occupations as a classed as well as gendered process. This final ambition, to look at both gender and class as they intersect with occupation, is not a trivial undertaking. As Castree et al. (2004: 55 in McDowell, 2008; 21) argue: 'the specific way that class and non-class differences articulate is complex' and this has led to an absence of theorising of the intersections of class and gender. As McDowell (2008) notes, while there has been a resurgence of interest in class in social theory, the work that has been done neglects the intersections of gender and class (and age, ethnicity and sexuality) thereby simplifying inequality. While this book takes gender, class and occupation rather than other social divisions as its focus, it hopes to begin to address this issue of intersectionality. Furthermore, McDowell (2008) also comments that much of the recent literature on class focuses on the working class – this book hopes to provide a more detailed understanding of class experience by examining the interconnections and distances between multiple class positions.

## Structure

This book consists of two parts. The first part of the book provides an overview of the theoretical and methodological approaches I utilise. Chapter 2 explains my theoretical standpoint; it discusses the Bourdieusian approach that underpins this book. However, gender capital is not Bourdieu's concept. In this chapter I argue that, while Bourdieu's conceptual approach is the most useful for the analysis of class and occupation, it is also necessary to move beyond Bourdieu in order to see gender as central in social space and to account for change and ambivalence. Chapter 3 then provides an overview of the histories, demographics and cultures of the four occupations I have chosen as 'case studies' to explore the operation of gender capital. In doing so, I hope to provide a rationale for focussing on worker's experiences in nursing, social work, exotic dancing and hairdressing. Chapter 4 then outlines my methodological approach. This chapter discusses how

I collected and framed the data as well as how I located both the gender and class identities and positions of the workers who participated in my research.

The second part of the book shifts in focus to examine the workers' gendered and classed experiences, including their gender capital experiences within the four occupations.

Chapter 5 initiates the case study analysis and looks at the experiences of nursing workers. Chapter 6 explores an occupation that has much in common with nursing: social work. Chapter 7 moves away from middle-class professions and examines a very different job: exotic dancing. Chapter 8 discusses experiences in hairdressing, a job that appears to have more in common with exotic dancing than nursing and social work (despite its distance from the sex industry). And finally Chapter 9 draws conclusions and argues for the validity of this theoretical approach.

# 2
# Why Use Bourdieusian Theory to Study Gender, Class and Work? The Case for 'Gender Capital'

Pierre Bourdieu's primary intellectual concern was the role of culture in the production and reproduction of power and inequality. As Atkinson (2009) suggests, Bourdieu's analysis of cultural life has been widely influential and has inspired a 'cultural turn' in the theorisation of class. In particular, he moved beyond economic determinism to explore alternative forms of social and cultural wealth. In doing so he provided an understanding of class that progressed beyond stratification and focussed on practice; his approach allows an analysis of the individual and their unique, yet structured, class experiences. And while his primary intellectual concern was class, his conceptual toolkit has proven to be adaptable – making it suitable for the analysis of gender, class and occupation.

This chapter outlines my theoretical framework. First, I provide an overview of Bourdieu's key class concepts. Second, I look at Bourdieu's less extensive understanding of occupation; exploring how, due to his cultural focus, Bourdieu necessarily moved beyond the conceptualisation of occupation as category. Third, in the last section of the chapter, I discuss Bourdieu's limited understanding of gender and evaluate the significance of his concepts for studying gender relations and, more specifically, gender and work. In so doing I necessarily move *beyond* Bourdieu, introducing what might be considered a feminist Bourdieusian concept: gender capital. I propose that through this appropriation a better understanding of the interrelationship between gender, class and occupation may be developed.

## Bourdieu on class

Bourdieu's extensive theorising of class (rather than his conceptualisation of gender and occupation which are somewhat under-theorised in

8

this work) is particularly valuable for my research purposes. Bourdieu saw class as having both economic and symbolic dimensions and he rejected the notion that class could be established 'a priori' (Weininger, 2005: 85). Rather, the boundaries of class can only be understood in terms of social practice via empirical enquiry. Thus, as Weininger (2005: 115) argues, Bourdieu's approach is able 'to grasp the processes of "classmaking"'. And this is certainly the aim of this book – in its exploration of gender capital this book hopes to grasp some of the processes of classmaking; to explore how class and gender are articulated, made and reproduced in occupations.

Central to Bourdieu's vision of the social world is the concept of habitus. For Bourdieu (1990b: 72), to construct a theory of practice is to construct a 'theory of the mode of generation of practices', and the habitus is the source of this generation. The habitus is the internalisation of certain structures and histories and is a 'practice unifying and practice-generating principle' (Bourdieu, 1990a: 101). The habitus even frames bodily conduct so that 'social distinctions and practices are embedded in the most automatic gestures or the most insignificant techniques of the body – ways of walking or blowing one's nose, ways of eating and talking' (Bourdieu, 1984: 46).

Class groups possess 'homogeneity of the habitus' (Bourdieu, 1990a: 80). Objective structures are reproduced as 'durable dispositions' within individuals who experience similar material conditions (Bourdieu, 1990a: 85) and these classed dispositions engender aspirations and practices that are objectively attached to their particular class group (Bourdieu, 1990a: 77). This means that individual interactions and actions are always a component of larger class relations. The habitus creates action that appears 'sensible' and 'reasonable' for particular groups (Bourdieu, 1990a: 79). However, these common practices are not often consciously decided on by group members. Rather, they are adopted outside of discourse and consciousness, through bodily 'hexis' rather than mechanical learning (Bourdieu, 1990a: 88). Class habitus is 'harmonized without any intentional calculation or conscious reference to a norm and mutually adjusted *in the absence of any direct interaction* or, *a fortiori*, explicit co-ordination' (Bourdieu, 1990a: 80).

Therefore, there is a dialectic relationship between class dispositions and class positions. For Bourdieu, (1990a: 82) dispositions are 'so many marks of *social position* and hence social distance between objective positions'. In other words, relations of order structure both social structures and mental structures. It seems that most peoples' perceptions are based on hierarchical social divisions and for most individuals society tends to consist of 'them and us'. That is, we experience both physical and mental distance from others and 'social identity is defined and asserted through difference'. This constructing of difference, of 'them and us', is played out through commonplace understandings of the 'reasonable and unreasonable' and it is evident in everyday sayings such as 'that's not for the likes of us' (Bourdieu, 1984: 172; 1990a: 77). Hence, people classify *themselves* as well as others. This is the strength of the doxic order (a system of presuppositions that shape action in social fields (Benson and Neveu, 2005: 3)). In his major work on class, *Distinction*, Bourdieu (1984: 482) stated:

> The classifying subjects who classify the properties and practices of others, or their own, are also classifiable objects which classify themselves (in the eyes of others) by appropriating practices and properties that are already classified (as vulgar or distinguished, high or low, heavy or light etc – in other words, in the last analysis, as popular or bourgeois) according to their probable distribution between groups that are themselves classified.

These perceptions of the social world are not only acts of cognition; they are also acts of misrecognition. People recognise the social order in its most 'absolute' form and therefore exclude themselves from elements of social life that they are already excluded from (Bourdieu, 1984: 471). This is why Bourdieu (1984: 172) dismissed the idea that collective class consciousness may be 'awakened'; for this would only amount to the 'recognition of an order which is also established in the mind'.

The classificatory system, then, has the symbolic power to impose mental structures upon people (Bourdieu, 1984: 480). This 'symbolic violence' is the primary tool used to maintain the dominant order and produce class inequality. Power operates beneath direct institutional discrimination; it is exercised through and upon the bodies of individuals with their complicity (McNay, 2000: 36). Symbolic power therefore operates without physical force as if by 'magic' (Bourdieu, 2001: 38). Indeed, for Bourdieu, 'an institution can only be efficacious if it is objectified in bodies in the form of durable dispositions' (McNay, 2000: 36–7). Hence, Bourdieu's notion of power is similar to that of Foucault's in that domination is 'invisible' and 'gentle' and largely operates 'through the purely symbolic channels of communication and cognition (more precisely, misrecognition), recognition, or even feeling' (2001: 1–2).

Nevertheless, there is room for agency in Bourdieu's social world. Although the doxic system is indeed very effective, and although the actions of individuals who belong to class groups tend to be coordinated below consciousness, the practices that the habitus produces are also 'regulated improvisations' (Bourdieu, 1990a: 78). The habitus is a *subjective* system of internalised structures. An individual possesses their own specific version of a collective history, so that their '*individual system of dispositions* may be seen as a *structural variant* of all the other group or class habitus, expressing the difference between trajectories and positions inside or outside the class' (Bourdieu, 1990a: 86). Moreover, for Bourdieu, these group norms are not prescriptive or constraining, rather, they are merely 'potentialities' (McNay, 2000: 40). This means that each classed individual has agency and an individual history and trajectory.

An important element of social distinction is the presence or absence of capital. This, of course, means that different classes possess different volumes of capital (Bourdieu, 2001: 114). Bourdieu generally referred to three types of capital: economic, social and cultural capital, and in this way he recognised that there is symbolic as well as economic or material wealth in society (Murdock, 2000: 134). Economic capital is quite simply economic wealth; it is money and all goods that may be directly converted into money and it can be institutionalised through property rights (Bourdieu, 1986; 47). Social capital is the 'connections', social networks or social relations that come into play in class formation and passing on various forms of advantage (Honneth, 2000: 8). Social capital is constituted by social obligations and it is sometimes convertible into economic capital and may also be institutionalised in noble titles (Bourdieu, 1986: 47). Cultural capital is the most complicated species of capital as it takes three forms: it exists in the objectified state (in pictures, books, instruments etc.), in the institutionalised state (in the form of educational qualifications) and most importantly for the issues addressed in this book, in the embodied state so that it is part of the habitus. When it exists in the embodied state, cultural capital takes 'the form of long-lasting dispositions of the mind and body' (Bourdieu, 1986: 47). Bourdieu stated that embodied cultural capital 'presupposes a process of embodiment, incorporation, which, insofar as it implies a labour of inculcation and assimilation, costs time, time which must be invested personally by the investor' (1986: 49); this mean that it is sometimes the product of self-improvement but it may also be possessed without being deliberately cultivated (by virtue of socialisation etc.) (Bourdieu, 1986: 47–9).

Each of Bourdieu's capitals has the potential to be transformed into another type of capital (for example cultural capital might be transformed into economic capital) (Reay, 2004: 58) and, when legitimated, each of these capitals may also become *symbolic capital*. Symbolic capital is 'the prestige or recognition which various capitals acquire by virtue of *being* recognized and "known" as legitimate' (Lawler, 1999: 6); symbolic capital is therefore powerful capital. Although all types of capital may be converted to symbolic capital, embodied cultural capital has the best chance at achieving this status:

> Because the social conditions of its transmission and acquisition are more disguised than those of economic capital, it is predisposed to function as symbolic capital, i.e., to be unrecognized as capital and recognized as legitimate competence, as authority exerting an effect of (mis)recognition.
>
> (Bourdieu, 1986: 49)

However, for Bourdieu the legitimation of capital is achieved via symbolic violence – symbolic capital is attributed to certain practices as a consequence of the misperception of social space to the advantage of the dominant so that only the competencies and tastes of the middle class and upper class are attributed 'honour' (Lawler, 1999: 6, Weininger, 2005) and working-class mannerisms, language and modes of dress are deprived of symbolic power within the wider social field. For this reason we mock 'bogans' and 'chavs' and delight in the social in competencies of television characters like Kath and Kim and Vicky Pollard.[1] Nevertheless, it is important to note that the relative value of each type of capital varies from field to field (although they are valid in all fields). This means that working-class tastes and consumption choices do hold value within their own class group (although they probably will not provide power or status outside of that particular group).

Hence, according to Bourdieu, class is not only defined by an agent's position in relations of production, it is also lived out through the lifestyle and consumption 'choices' a person makes (what Bourdieu calls practices of distinction) (Bourdieu, 1984: 483). Moreover, these consumption and lifestyle 'choices' are not only delimited by material constraints, they are also made in accordance with cultural competence (Murdock, 2000: 135). Cultural competence refers to the habitus' 'capacity to produce classifiable practices and works and the capacity to differentiate and appreciate these practices and products' (Bourdieu, 1984: 170). Class harmony in habitus translates to a 'harmony of ethos and tastes' (Bourdieu, 1990a: 82). Murdock suggests that there are three elements to cultural competence: 'knowledge about the legitimate stock of cultural capital, mastery of the intellectual and social skills surrounding its consumption and use, and the ability to deploy this knowledge and skill to advantage in social situations' (2000: 135).

The education system also plays a key role in the production of inequality and distinction. For example, cultural competence is reproduced via educational institutions. Further, the education system is a key player in defining cultural capital (Murdock, 2000: 135–6). In defining what is, and is not, symbolic and cultural capital, the education system commits acts of symbolic violence. The education system's definition of cultural capital conforms to, and supports, elite culture and competencies. Moreover, schools treat academic success as 'innate giftedness', differences in success are presented as '*individual* differences' and structural inequalities are not addressed (Murdock, 2000: 137). This further legitimates the inequitable distribution of capital within society (Murdock, 2000: 138). In addition the family plays a part in the reproduction of cultural competencies and it is via the family that the transmission of the primary habitus and cultural capital takes place. According to Bourdieu 'it is from the family that children derive modes of thinking, types of dispositions, sets of meaning and qualities of style' (Reay, 2004: 58) and this primarily occurs through socialisation. These dispositions and attributes are then accorded a cultural value by the dominant groups.

The distribution of capital endows people with particular positions within a network of objective relations. Bourdieu termed these networks 'fields'. Each field has a relationship with other fields, however, each field is also governed by an independent logic and that logic is 'irreducible' to the logic that regulates other fields (for example, the artistic field does not operate in the same way as the economic field). Bourdieu compared the field to a game that follows rules and regularities that are not directly explicit. The agents who are operating in these fields are players who are engaged in this game and hold particular 'stakes' within it. Each player holds particular tokens (particular types of capital) that are of a particular volume and structure that they use in competition with others. These tokens determine the moves each player makes and the positions they take up.

However, the relative value of each type of capital varies from field to field (although they are valid in all fields) (Bourdieu and Wacquant, 1992: 97–9) and even though these networks of relations often assume a relative stability, the struggle for the accumulation of capital within each field's particular game means that fields are characterised by conflict. Moreover, groups struggle to transform the rules of the game. For example, classes struggle to discredit the capital of their opponents or to give greater value to the capital that their particular group tends to possess (Bourdieu and Wacquant, 1992: 99). Working-class individuals who express pride in being working class or disapproval of certain 'airs and graces' can be seen to be engaging in this type of struggle. This struggle and movement within fields means that while 'people do tend to cluster together in the social space in more or less distinct "clouds" there are actually 'no hard and fast boundaries between classes' (Atkinson, 2009: 903). What is more, there is movement *between* fields so that individuals can diverge from class destiny. Bourdieu (1984: 111) stated that members of any given class will deviate from their class trajectory and follow the trajectory of a different class. Class mobility may occur through the re-conversion of capital. One form of capital may be converted to a 'more accessible, more profitable or more legitimate form' and hence transform an 'asset structure' (Bourdieu, 1984: 131). This acknowledgement of the possibilities for movement no doubt arises from the fact that Bourdieu himself deviated from his working-class origins and rose to the apex of French society. Indeed, in his autobiographical reflections he noted that his is a 'split habitus' and this enabled his critique of French society (Krais, 2006: 130).

## Bourdieu on class and occupations: a cultural analysis

Where do occupations fit within Bourdieu's analysis of social space and in particular, his analysis of class? In his article, *Rethinking the Work-Class Nexus*, Will Atkinson (2009) provides a detailed interpretation of Bourdieu's approach to work and occupations. Atkinson (2009: 902) argues that despite the assertions of Weiniger (2005: 86ff) and Bourdieu's early work with Boltanski (1981) on the space of posts, Bourdieu did not see social space as 'a space of occupations or an occupational structure'. As Bourdieu's approach to class is a cultural one, he did not see occupation as necessarily standing in for class in the way that the popular 'employment aggregate approach' that was instigated by Marx and Weber did (Crompton, 1998 cited in Atkinson, 2009: 898). Rather, the social space was conceptualised by Bourdieu more broadly, as a space of social relations. As I discussed in the previous section of this chapter, for Bourdieu, classes are not determined by substantial properties like occupation; classes are relational. People are clustered in 'clouds' in social space and their class is defined in terms of the distance between them, their personal (but collective) histories and the directions in which they are heading (Atkinson, 2009: 903). This means that all people, whether they are in paid employment or not, are classed subjects.

Nevertheless, Bourdieu did (1987: 4) argue that occupation 'remains a good and economic indicator of position in social space' (cited in Atkinson, 2009: 903). Atkinson (2009: 903) suggests that this is particularly the case for quantitative research, because an occupation 'requires a certain amount and structure of capital – certain occupations require a certain level and type of education, occupations are paid differently and so on'. Occupations therefore have particular economic and cultural characteristics and for this reason 'clouds of individuals ... tend to correspond roughly with certain types of occupations – intellectual-creative, public sector, business, manual work, clerical work and so on' (Atkinson, 2009; 903). Indeed, Atkinson asserts that this is partly why Bourdieu's social space is formed into clouds: 'certain occupational types require and distribute similar capital rewards which are markedly different from other occupational types' (2009: 903–4). This is also why trajectory is significant for understanding class: sections of social space 'rise or fall' as the state of play for particular occupations changes (for example as they become professionalised, lose respectability or experience pay cuts) (Atkinson, 2009: 903–4).

Furthermore, on a qualitative level, work shares a relationship with class in that it can impact an individual's habitus through 'occupational effects' (Bourdieu, 1987: 4 cited in Atkinson, 2009: 904). Bourdieu argued that 'the working conditions and the general milieu' can produce different habitus' and he provided the example of the 'workshop versus the office' (1984: 438, 447, cited in Atkinson, 2009: 904). Although they may not be fields in themselves, different type of work have certain cultures and operate in certain environments and these cultures and environment can have a structuring effect on the habitus – they may even assist in creating fairly homogenous habituses in co-workers. This means that the 'spatio-temporal and organizational structure' of forms of work can impact a person's disposition (Atkinson, 2009: 904).

Atkinson reflects further on this last point. Atkinson (2009) provides examples of how work environments can impact both classed *and* gendered dispositions. For example, if masculine spheres of work are physically demanding, practical and take place in 'hard' environments, those who participate in this work (mostly men) will come to embody the environment, develop practical competencies and develop strength as if they are natural. This is how these types of work further produce hegemonic masculinity. Moreover, if mostly working-class men occupy these areas of work, the environment can also accentuate their class dispositions; a very good 'fit' is eventually developed between physically demanding work and working-class dispositions.

Thus, particular work dispositions become working-class masculinity rather than middle-class masculinity. In addition, Atkinson (2009: 905) discusses how the temporal experience of contract work may also complicate or enhance class dispositions; in that it reinforces a 'live for the moment' type of attitude (that other theorists such as Connell (1991) have associated with working-class masculinity), that is not necessarily prevalent among individuals who are paid an annual income and have access to promotion. It is not only the manual, non-manual divide that produces different types of workers. The 'cultural and organizational specificities' of occupations might also impact individuals' habitus' (Bourdieu, 1987: 4, cited in Atkinson, 2009: 905). There are different categories of professional work, manual work, emotional work and so forth which means that class (and I would add gender) might be played out very differently depending whether a person is a nurse, secretary, engineer or carpenter. Atkinson (2009: 905) adds that at the most micro-level, local workplace cultures (that vary between shops, companies, institutions etc.) may produce differently articulated habituses depending on the interactions, norms and behaviours that are produced in each specific space.

Bourdieu conceptualises occupations as occupying social space. Atkinson (2009: 907) argues:

> because occupations going under the same name, with similar tasks, can remunerate to relatively variable levels and require variable levels of credentials, they occupy *spaces* with a greater or lesser spread over social space. Witness the diagrams in *Distinction* (1984: 262, 340), displaying correspondence analyses of different sections of social space, in which we see that the (analytical) boundaries of particular occupational categories range over regions of different shapes and sizes and even overlap.

Those who work within particular occupations are loosely clustered in similar spaces and in this way they share a kind of social proximity. However, their locations in social space are not exactly the same. Their locations vary depending upon their positions within the occupations' hierarchy as well as the level and composition of each individual's capitals. In other words, 'there is enough dispersion to recognise the internal heterogeneity of occupational groups, even if there is still, analytically, a central hub of the occupational group – a mean position – around which the individuals swarm' (Atkinson, 2009: 907–8).

In addition, as I stated previously, occupations are not fields exactly, 'as they fail to display the criteria necessary to describe them as such – for example, common stakes, struggle and competition etc. They are, however, affected by the existence of fields and people's places and strategies within them, whether the field of power (Bourdieu, 1984), the field of higher education institutions (Bourdieu, 1996), the journalistic field (Bourdieu, 1998), the field formed by a large employer (Bourdieu, 2005), or whatever' (Atkinson, 2009: 910). This is seen, for example, when occupations fight to be accredited in higher education.

Hence, in Bourdieu's schema, the relationship between class and occupation is both significant and complex. Occupation is not a reliable indicator of class as occupations are not intrinsically attached to a class even though they might perpetuate capital. This is because they are not the only source of capital and 'class dispositions are separable from occupational effects' (Atkinson, 2009: 906). However, it could be argued that occupations may 'be useful indicators of some elements of capital' and Atkinson asserts that according to a Bourdieusian approach, occupations and work dispositions:

> add to, complicate and articulate the general class dispositions built out of greater and lesser distance from necessity and cultural conditions and an understanding of this link is crucial to qualitative work aiming to grasp the interplay of the general and more specific in shaping action and subjectivity.
>
> (2009: 905)

This means that researching work may provide insights into the structure of class habituses. Although Bourdieu advocated a cultural approach to class, this does not mean that his insights are not useful for studying occupations or that occupations are not significant for class analysis.

## Bourdieu on gender

How does gender fit into Bourdieu's analysis of class? Bourdieu (1984: 107) famously stated that 'sexual properties are as inseparable from class properties as the yellowness of a lemon is from its acidity'. In other words, class is always gendered; class and gender are intimately connected. Yet, despite this acknowledgement of the inseparability of gender and class, gender is largely under-theorised in Bourdieu's work. It seems that although his theorising of class was comprehensive and groundbreaking, Bourdieu was 'gender blind'; in most of his writings class is *the* primary organising structure in social space. Moreover, Bourdieu tended to privilege male and masculine experience. For example, Silva (2005: 86–7) shows how Bourdieu saw the 'social origin' of his respondents in his *Distinction* study as patrilinear; he asked questions about the educational qualifications and occupations of the fathers and grandfathers rather than the women in families. She also finds that, apart from the new 'petite bourgeoise', women were not adequately represented in the survey sample.

However, in 2001, quite late in his academic career, Bourdieu published *Masculine Domination* in which he clearly attempted to rectify these shortcomings. In *Masculine Domination* Bourdieu undertook a considerable rethinking of the applicability of his concepts for the analysis of gender. Within this work, Bourdieu (1990, 2001) replicated the basic argument he made in *Distinction* but explicitly addressed gender as a principle organisational feature in social space (Silva, 2005: 89). As the title suggests, his focus in this text is on domination – gender domination. Here he revisited his data from his earlier work on Kabyle and reflected on Virginia Woolf's (1927) fiction *To the Lighthouse* (which he proposed provides a particularly lucid account of the contradictions of the masculine experience of masculine domination) to explore the reproduction of the gender order.

*Masculine Domination* is similar to Bourdieu's other works on the symbolic order and social practice; in that the habitus plays a central role. In this text gender dispositions are embodied in the habitus so that gender relations are ever present in 'perception, thought and action' (Bourdieu, 2001: 8). The gendered habitus is constructed '*relationally*'; in that it is '*socially differentiated* from the opposite gender' (Bourdieu, 2001: 23–4); the female habitus is constructed in cultural opposition to the male habitus and the male habitus is constructed in cultural opposition to the female habitus. Bourdieu (2001) asserted that the habitus assures consistency in practice over time so that gendered dispositions often appear to be relatively stable. As it does with class, the habitus assures an innate complacency that shapes gender 'aspirations according to concrete indices of the accessible and the inaccessible, of what is and what is not "for us"' (Bourdieu, 1990: 64). The habitus therefore assures relative consistency in what is considered masculine and what is considered feminine.

The body plays an important part in the production of gender difference. As with the class system, gender binaries are lived out through *bodily hexis* in facial expression, body shape and deportment. Gender is an inscription of 'collective expectations' on the body (Bourdieu, 2001: 61). The body is therefore 'a thinking animal'; Bourdieu highlights the 'somatic expression of the political' (Fowler, 2003: 471). However, gender is unique to other forms of social classification and distinction; in that the gender order and gendered practices also 'have their material point of reference in the human activities related to sexuality and the reproduction of human life' and bodily differences between men and women play a central role in these activities (Krais, 2006: 120–1).

In her article, *Gender, Sociological Theory and Bourdieu's Sociology of Practice*, Beate Krais argues that this reference to bodily differences between men and women 'constitutes a crucial difference between the symbolic order of gender and other social classifications such as class or nation' (2006: 121). This reference to bodily difference means that social differences between men and women are interpreted as natural differences, and notions of masculinity and femininity are often deeply entrenched (McNay, 2000: 37–41). Like no other structure, the gender order, 'makes us forget that it is itself a social structure, produced and reproduced by humans themselves' (Krais, 2006: 121).

Hence, the gender order is particularly entrenched because masculine domination is predominantly legitimated, '*by embedding it in a biological nature that is itself a naturalised social construct*' (Bourdieu, 2001: 23, italics in original). Women as well as men are complicit in this gendered classification of the world. As McNay (2000: 37) states, 'women become implicated within a circular logic where the culturally arbitrary is imposed upon the body in a naturalized form whose cognitive effects (*doxa*) result in the further naturalization of arbitrary social differences' (McNay, 2000: 37). This is how domination operates: a gendered 'doxic order' is shared by the dominated and the dominant. Hegemonic images of binary oppositions shape stereotypes – they shape how women are and men are perceived and how they perceive themselves.

Bourdieu argued that this gender order can be to the detriment to both women *and* men. Following Marx, and drawing on examples from Virginia Woolf's *To the Lighthouse*, Bourdieu (2001: 69) suggested that men are also 'dominated by their domination'. Although men tend to be empowered with 'world-making' in that 'they monopolise the most delicate and prestigious of human inventive actions' they also 'trap *themselves* by the possibility of ignominy and ridicule' (Fowler, 2003: 472–3). Hence, for Bourdieu (2001: 75), masculine domination is experienced by the dominant as a 'double-edged privilege'.

As with the class system, the use of symbolic violence is the primary means by which the gender order is maintained. According to Bourdieu

(2001) gendered 'visions and divisions' of the world are constructed by those with legitimate authority. Those who do not have this authority must see themselves in the 'actions and discourses of others' (Mahar, Harker and Wilkes, 1990: 14). According to Krais (2006: 121), while the concept of symbolic violence and symbolic domination is present in his other writing, *Masculine Domination* is where its analytical potential becomes clearest. In *Masculine Domination* 'symbolic violence manifests its power essentially in *face-to-face* interactions: it constitutes and reproduces domination in the immediate interactions between people' (Krais, 2006: 121, italics in original). Bourdieu (2001: 42) stated that symbolic violence is manifested in 'injunctions, suggestions, seduction, threats, reproaches, orders or calls to order'; symbolic violence provides these everyday acts with a 'hypnotic power'.

It seems then, in Masculine Domination, as in Bourdieu's other works, Bourdieu's primary concern is the *reproduction* of the symbolic order. Bourdieu stressed the consistency of non-rational patterns of gender action but also the 'longevity, subtlety and emotional power of gender oppositions' (Fowler, 2003: 474). Therefore his theories are, as Fowler (2003: 486) describes, 'realist'. Bourdieu explained the difficulties of change and the role that many women play in the perpetuation of masculine domination. For example, Bourdieu argued that as the manner in which gender is lived out is largely subconscious or pre-reflexive, 'the destabilizing of conventional gender relations on one level may further entrench, in a reactive fashion, conventional patterns of behaviour on other levels' (McNay, 2000: 41). This means that Bourdieu's theory is most appropriate for understanding why gender segregation might persist in a workforce that has established anti-discrimination policies, as well as for studying pre-reflexive masculine and feminine behaviour such as 'machoness' and 'mothering', and in this way his approach runs counter to recent theories of reflexive transformation (such as Giddens' theory of the transformation of intimacy) which emphasise conscious self-awareness (McNay, 2000: 41).

Of course, Bourdieu has been widely critiqued for precisely this – his focus on the reproduction of symbolic orders. As feminists are politically invested in researching and creating possibilities for change in gender relations, many have disapproved of Bourdieu's approach. These critiques tend to focus on the habitus concept; the habitus is seen as 'deterministic, and thus incapable of both taking into account the individual's reflexivity and comprehending processes of social change (cf. E.g. Calhoun; Butler, 1999)' (Krais, 2006: 120). One of the most notable objections to Bourdieu's approach has come from Judith Butler.

Butler (1997) asserts that because Bourdieu does not see speech as having the power to resignify unless it has authorisation, his approach results in a base/superstructure model.

However, against Butler Bourdieu has argued (2001: 103) that gender is not merely a role that can be 'abolished by an act of performative magic', for it is 'inscribed in bodies and in a universe from which they derive their strength'. Several Bourdieusian feminists have also defended Bourdieu on this point (for example, see Adkins, 2004; McNay, 2000). Fowler (2003: 477) argues that Bourdieu did stress the subjective makings of class classifications and representations. Also, with reference to Butler's example of transgressive performance, Fowler (2003: 478) shows that 'charismatic figures like Rosa Parks can only create new 'prophetic' messages 'because, as leading figures, they were emblematic of the group's own deepest aspirations. Their own politically prophetic habitus has become objectively attuned to the degraded and stigmatized character of the addressed masses'.

And although Bourdieu focussed on reproduction in his analysis of gender as with his analysis of class, there are moments when he discussed change. Bourdieu (2001) asserted that, despite the strength of the doxic order and the persuasive nature of symbolic violence, the doxic order can be contested. Women's consciousness does not necessarily form around the acceptance of the social order as self-evident. Bourdieu stated that 'there is always room for cognitive struggle over the meaning of things of the world and in particular of sexual realities' (2001: 13–14). For Bourdieu, the existence of domination implies the existence of resistance (McNay, 1999: 99). And the marginalised are particularly capable of reflexive activity; Bourdieu 'is always aware that there are women who are "lucid outsiders", whose own angle of vision allows them to break with the habitus of the powerless female, at whatever cost' (Fowler, 2003: 486).

Nevertheless, while Bourdieu is sometimes overly criticised, perhaps *Masculine Domination* should have placed greater emphasis on uncertainty and change. As Krais (2006) points out, this limitation might have been overcome if *Masculine Domination* drew on data from contemporary society. Bourdieu fell short when he limited his analysis to his material from Kabylia and Virginia Woolf's *To the Lighthouse* as these are examples of perfectly neat and ordered worlds and contemporary Western society is not like this. Rather, contemporary Western society is complex and differentiated and simultaneously stagnant and changing. Krais (2006: 123–4) asserts that the contemporary gender order is a 'field of open political struggle' and 'in this struggle, women exist not only as *objects* but also as *social subjects*, agents who act in their own rights and in defence of their own interests'. In addition, as Fowler (2003: 474) states, 'Bourdieu has neglected the occasions when patriarchal domination has been publicly opposed; for example the forcible ending of the male monopoly over medicine (Witz, 1992)'. Moreover, in modern, differentiated society men and women occupy masculinity and femininity in ambiguous ways; there are multiple subjectivities. Yet, as McNay finds, because Bourdieu based his analysis in Kabyle society he tended to refer to a 'pure dualism of sexual difference' (2000: 53).

McNay (2000: 51) argues that Bourdieu's tendency to emphasise reproduction at the expense of change does not point to a problem that is inherent in his concepts per se. Rather, McNay (2000: 51) argues that his tendency to overemphasise the power of the symbolic order is due to his failure to satisfactorily integrate the concepts of habitus and symbolic violence with the concept of field. In fact, McNay (2000: 51) asserts that when the concept of field is given due consideration, Bourdieu provides a superior, more nuanced account of power and agency. Yet, Bourdieu did not include the concept of field in his discussion of masculine domination. Bourdieu considered the destabilising effects that may occur from movement across fields in his other works but does not look at the impact of field on the gendered habitus. McNay (2000: 53) found one point in *La noblesse d'Etat* where Bourdieu did mention 'the correlation between women's increased entry into higher education and declining levels of fertility' but he did not consider the broader implications this may have for gender identity.

Unfortunately, there are also other places where Bourdieu's analysis of gender relations falls short. In *Masculine Domination* Bourdieu failed to research by his own epistemological rules, and gain objectivity by creating distance between himself and his object of analysis. As Krais (2006: 123) points out, he failed to examine his position in relation to those who are concerned by the object of his research; he failed to interrogate his own masculine position.

Bourdieu omitted the reflexive process whereby, according to his own reasoning, a researcher must reconstruct the standpoints of others and in doing so describe the particularities of his or her own position (Krais, 2006: 123). Krais (2006: 123) suggests that if Bourdieu stayed true to his own epistemological process, he would have conducted a thorough reading of feminist research and thereby recognised 'his feminist colleagues as "equal players" in the intellectual field'. Instead, as Silva

(2005: 93) argues, 'the absence of the rich field of feminist work on the body is noticeable' in Bourdieu's analysis.

Bourdieu has also been critiqued for not acknowledging that women as well as men are classed subjects (see Krais, 2006; Lovell, 2000: McNay, 2004; Silva, 2005). Again, he has largely treated women as objects rather than subjects. Unfortunately, in all of his writings Bourdieu tended to conceptualise women as capital-bearing objects rather than capital-bearing subjects (Lovell, 2000: 21). As Silva points out, in *Masculine Domination* Bourdieu reaffirmed an idea put forward in *Distinction*: that in the matrimonial market women exist as objects, 'whose function is to contribute to the perpetuation or expansion of the symbolic capital held by men' (Bourdieu 2001: 43)' (2005: 96). Hence, Bourdieu tended to see women as contributing to the accumulation of capital for men rather than having capital accumulating strategies of their own. Women are mere 'repositories' of capital while men are the subjects of exchange (Lovell, 2000: 22; McNay, 2004: 142). In this way, although he stated that this naturalisation of the gender and class order through normal family arrangements and so forth is fiction, 'he falls terribly short of engaging with normal life, blinded by his own fiction' (Silva, 2005: 97).

However, Bourdieu's view on women's relationships with capital was not always clear. Although Bourdieu had a *tendency* to view women as objects rather than subjects of the class system, it must be recognised that in *Distinction* he did occasionally contradict himself on this matter. In *Distinction*, Bourdieu (1984: 206) mentioned in passing that petit-bourgeois women are aware of the market value of beauty and are particularly invested in beauty capital. Therefore, these women actively cultivate their bodies accordingly. In addition, Bourdieu mentioned that 'certain women derive occupational profit from their charm(s), and that beauty has acquired a value on the labour market' (1984: 152–3). Hence, although it is frustrating that he did not expand on these revelations in *Masculine Domination*, Bourdieu did recognise that it is in fact possible that women (like men) engage in the accumulation of capital and actively use it to their advantage.

But this is not all. I would like to suggest that perhaps the most disappointing element of *Masculine Domination* is a related issue. Within *Distinction* Bourdieu acknowledged the inseparability of gender and class; he demonstrated how 'anxieties about class status and belonging are sublimated into and played out through the categories of masculinity and femininity, thereby entrenching them further (1979: 382)' (McNay, 2000: 43). Yet, as Fowler (2003: 480) highlights, in *Masculine Domination*

Bourdieu treated 'women's oppression as analytically independent of class'. If his proposition from *Distinction* is true, if sexual properties are indeed 'as inseparable from class properties as the yellowness of a lemon is from its acidity', this is a serious oversight.

## Moving with, against and beyond Bourdieu: feminists rework capital

As the discussion thus far has indicated, there are a number of places where Bourdieu's work on gender is ambivalent or falls short. However, this does not mean that his theoretical approach is of no use to feminist researchers. Rather, feminists have responded to these shortfalls by *appropriating* Bourdieu's theoretical tools. Feminist appropriation is to give 'a critical assessment of a given theory formation with a view to take it over and use it for feminist purposes' (Moi, 1991: 1017). Toril Moi argues that a feminist approaching Bourdieu necessarily asks 'whether his major concepts can be simply applied to gender or whether they require rethinking and restructuring in order to become usable for her purposes. She will also have to raise the question of social change' (1991: 1020).

Of particular interest for this discussion, some Bourdieusian feminists have appropriated the capital concept in order to explore the research themes of gender and class and the relationship between gender and class in contemporary settings (see for example Lawler, 1999; Reay, 2004; Skeggs, 1997). In 'Getting Out and Getting Away: Women's Narratives of Class Mobility', Steph Lawler (1999) utilises the concept of habitus and cultural and symbolic capital in order to understand women's class mobility. Lawler examines seven women's narrations of their movement from working-class to middle-class positions to understand the difficulties of 'class success' and 'the pain and sense of estrangement associated with this class movement' (Lawler, 1999: 3). Bourdieu's concepts enable such an understanding because they facilitate an exploration of the 'cultural and symbolic configurations of class' (Lawler, 1999: 3). Here Lawler (1999) finds that if both the cultural and symbolic are considered, mobility no longer appears straightforward. For example, women's working-class histories tend to be treated as pathological and embodied, making them impossible to escape. Moreover, because the working class are recognised as pathological there is risk in attempting 'middle-classness' – there is risk of 'getting it wrong' or appearing pretentious (Lawler, 1999: 3).

Other feminists and social theorists have actually expanded upon Bourdieu's species and subtypes of capital (see for example, Illouz (1997), Lovell (2000), McCall (1992), Reay (2004), Shilling (1991) and Skeggs (2004)). Although there is beauty in the simplicity of Bourdieu's original three-part approach (comprising of economic, cultural and social capital), Bourdieu himself suggested the evolutionary potential of his framework when he added symbolic capital to his formulation and when he proposed that each species has subtypes (see Bourdieu and Wacquant, 1992: 119). Furthermore, there is value in expanding Bourdieu's formulation as, (in Bourdieu's own words) 'acknowledging that capital can take a variety of forms is indispensable to explain the structure and dynamics of differentiated societies' (Bourdieu and Wacquant, 1992: 119). Differentiating new forms of capital enables theorists to provide a deeper understanding of wealth and inequality.

Significantly, feminists have recently developed the concept 'gendered capital'. Most notably, in the early 1990s in an article titled 'Does Gender Fit? Feminism, Bourdieu, and Conceptions of Social Order' feminist sociologist Leslie McCall (1992) proposed that gender is a cultural capital. Although Bourdieu originally saw gender as a secondary form of stratification and therefore depicted capital as gender neutral and merely shaped by gender in the 'reconversion process' (McCall, 1992: 841–2), McCall (1992: 843) states that an argument for gendered capital can actually be grounded in Bourdieu's formulation of embodied cultural capital. As I argued earlier, Bourdieu proposed that cultural capital is sometimes embodied – that dispositions operate as forms of capital. This means that gender dispositions might also be a form of capital (McCall, 1992). Furthermore, as McCall (1992: 842–4) points out, Bourdieu did not term gender 'secondary' only on the basis of its significance in stratification, gender was also termed 'secondary' due to its hidden form. This allows for an interpretation of gender as a primary, yet elusive, social force which appears as natural and universal; it opens up the possibility for gender to be a significant form of capital (McCall, 1992: 842).

Beverley Skeggs' (1997) *Formations of Class and Gender* expands on this understanding of gendered capital. In Skeggs' (1997: 7) view 'capital' best enables an explanation of 'the intersections of gender and class in subject production'. Skeggs (1997) employs Bourdieu's theory of class in order to understand the classed experiences of 83 working-class women who participated in caring courses at a further education college. Skeggs (1997) finds that the participants made particular investments in femininity and, in response to negative representations of the working class, were committed to the achievement of respectability. These women were therefore actively pursuing capital; however, they did not have the type of capital that could be converted into money and symbolic capital, rather 'they were in the process of continually halting losses rather than trading-up and accruing extra value' (Skeggs, 1997: 161). Furthermore, these investments in femininity were generally useful only at the local level and often involved closing off other possibilities for themselves (Skeggs, 1997: 161).

Skeggs (1997) therefore found that these women possess their own *feminine* forms of capital (although feminine capital may also be used by men and masculine capital may also be used by women (Skeggs, 2004: 24)). Femininity, particularly hegemonic femininity or stereotypical femininity, is culturally learnt and may operate as a form of cultural capital. Skeggs (1997: 10) argues that femininity as cultural capital 'is the discursive position available through gender relations that women are encouraged to inhabit and use. Its use will be informed by the network of social positions of class, gender, sexuality, region, age and race which ensure that it will be taken up (and resisted) in different ways'. Furthermore, in her chapter 'Context and Background: Pierre Bourdieu's Analysis of Class, Gender and Sexuality', Skeggs (2004: 24) argues that the concept of capital may be reworked further so that we may see the use-value of the various femininities that are other than upper-middle-class femininity. Skeggs (2004: 24) proposes that this reworking could take place if we think about other forms of culture, rather than just high culture, as a resource. If this were to take place, then capital would be extended beyond 'high cultural practices and classifications', it could also be separated 'from the fields and means by which it is *exchanged*' (Skeggs, 2004: 24). For Skeggs (2004: 24) then, gender 'can be a range of things; it can be a resource, a form of regulation, an embodied disposition and/or a symbolically legitimate form of capital'.

In her chapter titled 'Gendering Bourdieu's Concepts of Capitals? Emotional Capital, Women and Social Class' Diane Reay (2004) draws on Eva Illouz (1997) to explore the possibilities of another capital that has not been identified by Bourdieu: emotional capital. Reay (2004) argues that Bourdieu largely overlooked emotions within his work and attempts to redress this oversight within her chapter, utilising research into mothers' involvement in their children's education to develop the concept of emotional capital. For Reay (2004: 71), emotional capital 'is all about investments in others rather than the self'. Moreover, emotional capital is largely drawn upon by women, and although both working-class and middle-class women invest intensively in their children's education, emotional capital is both gendered and classed. For example, Reay found that it was more difficult for the working-class women in her study to provide this emotional involvement because they experienced other distracting concerns that were related to their class position (for example, poverty). Working-class women also experienced greater difficulty than middle-class women in diverting this emotional involvement into educational gain for their children. Reay (2004: 65) states that 'working-class women often lacked the right condition or context for providing either emotional or dominant cultural capital'; emotional well-being is less likely to be achieved in situations of poverty. In sum, Reay argues that emotional capital is 'one capital that is useful for unravelling some of the confusing class and gender processes embedded in contemporary educational markets' (2004: 71). Indeed, I would like to propose that because emotional competency is closely associated with hegemonic notions of femininity so that emotional competency and femininity are seen as one and the same, emotional capital might even be understood as a gender capital: a feminine capital. This idea will be explored in more detail later in this book.

Elsewhere, in 'Reworking Bourdieu's "Capital": Feminine and Female Capitals in the Field of Paid Caring Work', I also argue that both feminine capital and *female* capital exist (Huppatz, 2009). Women's advantage therefore takes form in two different types of gender capital. Drawing on my research into women's careers in paid caring work I argue that while femininity certainly can be an asset, the concepts of 'femininity' and 'female' should not be conflated so that femininity is generalised as a female condition. Female capital is the gender advantage that is derived from being perceived to have a female (but not necessarily feminine) body and feminine capital is the gender advantage that is derived from a disposition or skill set learnt via socialisation, or from simply being hailed as feminine (this occurs when one's body is recognised as feminine). The concepts of feminine capital and female capital might be useful for understanding gendered occupational practices and in particular the way that gender inequality and privilege operate within particular types of work. Moreover, they may facilitate a better understanding of the intersections of gender, class and occupation.

Some theorists have argued against the expansion of Bourdieu's conceptual toolkit to include gender capital. For example, Bennett et al. (2009) argue that gender is not a capital, rather, it informs or structures cultural capital within fields. They have reservations about developing Bourdieu's original formula, suggesting that this is a project that will never end so that we will have a limitless list of wealth. However, I would like to assert that gender capital is a credible addition because it allows for an understanding of both class and gender processes; it makes gender central in social space. Thus, this reworking serves an important political function in addition to a theoretical and empirical purpose.

## Bourdieu on gender and occupations

As I discussed in the previous section of this chapter, in *Masculine Domination* Bourdieu was concerned with the reproduction of gendered dispositions and practices. Interestingly, he primarily illustrated this reproduction through discussions of women's experiences of paid work and he argued that women's labour market experiences show *'permanence in and through change'* (Bourdieu, 2001: 91, italics in original). Bourdieu asserted that the gendered symbolic order is evident in how women tend to be clustered in devalued, feminised work. It is also evident in how women tend to be disadvantaged in relation to men in obtaining prestigious positions in occupational hierarchies. Bourdieu argued that consistency in the gender order is evident in the way that the women who have succeeded in gaining prestige in the labour market have done so 'in the dominated regions in the field of power, that is, in the domain of the production and circulation of symbolic goods (publishing, journalism, the media, teaching etc.)' (2001: 92). These 'successful' women are therefore subordinate elites and they also have to pay a price for their positions; in that they must 'banish all sexual connotation from their bodily *hexis* and dress' (Bourdieu, 2001: 92–3).

Bourdieu argued that the old structures of the division between the genders seem to determine the direction of changes in gender relations because they are objectified in 'disciplines, careers and jobs' and they also 'act through *three practical principles* which women, and also their social circles, apply in their choices' (2001: 95). All of these principles are related to work. First, the jobs appropriate to women are 'an extension of their domestic functions – education, care and service'; second, 'women cannot have authority over men and so men are more likely to be promoted to positions of authority'; and third 'men monopolise "technical objects and machines"' (Bourdieu, 2001: 95). Gendered occupational segregation is the objectification of an unequal relationship between men and women and women's career choices are structured by this relationship as well.

Bourdieu therefore discussed the gendered habitus and the role that it plays in perpetuating the gendered division of labour. Just as with class, gendered individuals internalise the social order and limit themselves from activities. Bourdieu argued that 'The constancy of habitus that results from this is thus one of the most important factors in the relative constancy in the structure of the sexual division of labour' (2001: 95). Girls do not pursue careers that are not seen as 'natural' for women: 'refusing the courses or careers from which they are anyway excluded and rushing towards those for which they are in any case destined' (Bourdieu, 2001: 95).

In addition he asserted that the strong connections between positions and dispositions make it very difficult for masculinised occupations to accept women. Bourdieu argued:

> social positions themselves are sexually characterized, and character-
> izing, and ... in defending their jobs against feminization, men are
> trying to protect their most deep-rooted idea of themselves as men,
> especially in the case of social categories such as manual workers or
> occupations such as those of the army, which owe much, if not all
> their value, even in their own eyes, to their image of manliness.
>
> (Bourdieu, 2001: 96)

As I discussed earlier, certain jobs become associated with masculinity or femininity and there is an 'occupational effect' so that certain dispositions are even produced or become further pronounced through work environments. This means that those who have invested in normative gender identities may also be invested in retaining gendered occupations.

Occupations are also significant in Bourdieu's analysis of gender because, once again, just as with class, gender is not just a position – gender is a relational concept. So to understand gender the researcher must uncover 'the relation of domination between men and women as it establishes itself *in the whole set of social spaces and subspaces*' including, he argues, occupational spaces. This is because masculine domination is maintained 'beyond the *substantive* differences in condition linked to moments in history and positions in social space' (Bourdieu, 2001: 102, italics in original).

Furthermore, Bourdieu argued that the permanence of invisible structures can only be made visible through 'relational thinking capable of *making the connection between domestic economy and therefore the division of labour and powers which characterize it, and the various sectors of the labour market* (the fields) in which men and women are involved' (2001: 106). For example, successful executive women must pay for success in the public realm 'with less "success" in the domestic realm (divorce, late marriage or no marriage, difficulties or failures with children, etc.) and in the economy of symbolic goods' (Bourdieu, 2001: 107). Bourdieu argued that when you account for the constraints that the structure of domestic space brings upon the occupational space, it becomes possible to see the 'homology between the structures of the male positions and female positions in the various social spaces' (2001: 107).

Thus, as he primarily used illustrative examples from the world of work to explain gender relations and masculine domination, Bourdieu highlighted the role occupations play in this domination and provided a rationale for feminists to continue their focus on gender power and inequality in occupations. What is more, he demonstrated how his conceptual toolkit of habitus, doxa and symbolic violence is valuable for the analysis of occupations, and his understanding of the homology of gender positions both within work and outside of it is useful for analysing the relationship between gender and work.

Yet, once again, capital is largely absent from Bourdieu's discussion of gender and work. As I touched on in the previous section of this chapter, Bourdieu vaguely dealt with the relationship between women and capital when he argued that although women might be distanced from one another by economic and cultural factors, including occupation, and this may impact 'their objective and subjective ways of undergoing and suffering masculine domination', they nevertheless 'have in common the fact that they *are separated from men by a negative symbolic coefficient*' (2001: 93, italics in original). And for this reason, 'there is something common between a woman managing director ... and the woman production line worker' (Bourdieu, 2001: 93). Here he is arguing that all women experience diminished symbolic capital but this is the limit to his analysis. Again, this means that any feminist appropriation of Bourdieu must necessarily also move beyond Bourdieu.

## Gender Capital and the New Economy

In moving beyond Bourdieu, feminists have made connections between gendered capital and occupations. Indeed, several theorists have suggested that we are witnessing greater use of gender as capital in the labour market due to changes in the economy. For example, in her article *Thinking Feminism with and against Bourdieu*, Terry Lovell (2000) suggests that the labour market is changing so that the demand for stereotypical feminine skills is rising. Lovell (2000: 25) therefore argues that femininity may be tradable for economic capital on the labour market, just as masculinity is (although femininity may not be rewarded with symbolic capital) and this may mean that working-class femininity is becoming more profitable than working-class masculinity. In her article *The New Economy, Property and Personhood,* Lisa Adkins (2005) also suggests that there exists a 'new economy' in which gender is seen as a cultural product; as a malleable, indeterminable, workplace resource. However Adkins (2005) argues that gendered capital is limited by a reworking of the relationship between people and their labour. As work in this new economy increasingly involves social interaction and embodied performance, its profitability depends very much on 'audience effects' so that customer experience or customer satisfaction is a key indicator of employee performance. Adkins (2005: 124) suggests that this is particularly evident in relation to gender, as performances of femininity are often considered the outcome of 'natural advantages' and therefore customer effects are not necessarily made visible. For this reason Adkins (2005) proposes that people do not necessarily always own or accumulate gendered capital (and in this way Adkins (2005) also departs from Bourdieu – for Adkins (2005) gendered capital does not always 'stick' to the subject). Feminists have therefore proposed ways in which the capital concept can be reworked to understand changes in the labour market. The gender capital concept may therefore also assist in understanding gendered practices in occupations.

## Conclusions

This chapter has introduced the theoretical framework for this book. As I have outlined in this chapter, Bourdieu's insights into the workings of class are particularly developed. His approach to class will therefore be taken up in this book, particularly to study the relationship between class and occupational 'experience, dispositions, struggles and social difference and distance' (Atkinson, 2009: 909). However, as his approach to gender and gender and occupations is limited, it will be necessarily to move beyond Bourdieu. I will take up feminist reworkings of Bourdieu and in particular, I will ask 'what about the relationship between gender, capital and occupation?' In the case study chapters of this book I will explore how gender, including femininity, operates as capital in the feminised occupational spaces of nursing, social work, exotic dancing and hairdressing. Moreover, I will take on feminist critiques of Bourdieu's emphasis on the reproduction of social life and take note of gendered and classed performances as well as transgressions.

The next chapter will move on to outline the cultures, histories and demographics of the four occupations I have chosen to use as case studies for the examination of the intersections of gender, class and occupation, including the operation of gender capital. In doing so, it will provide a rationale for choosing these occupational spaces as case studies.

# 3
# Gender and Class in Four Occupations

This chapter reviews the history, culture and social dynamics of four feminised occupations that may be loosely defined as 'service jobs' as they exist in the UK and Australia: nursing, social work, exotic dancing and hairdressing. I have identified these jobs as service jobs because they involve caring for bodily needs, interacting with clients and embodied labour. In describing the histories, structures and characteristics of these occupations I hope to highlight the significance of both gendered and classed processes and identities for these occupations and therefore the applicability of Bourdieu's concepts for understanding these feminised areas of social action – in particular, for understanding how they continue to be open to some individuals but relatively closed to others, and how they serve to reinforce certain gendered and classed dispositions and positions. In doing this, I also hope to begin to establish an argument for why the concept 'gender capital' is significant for understanding individual's movements into and within these occupations.

I will start my discussion with nursing and social work – two paid 'caring occupations' – because it was in a study of these two occupations that my understanding of gender capital, and in particular, female and feminine capitals, was developed. Interestingly, historically, nursing and social work have been *constructed* as appropriate occupations for those who are of a particular gender and class; and I will argue that these two occupations continue to be middle class in population and culture. I will then move on to discuss the cultures and histories of exotic dancing and hairdressing, two feminised, working-class occupations.

# Nursing

Nursing was, and continues to be, actively constructed as 'women's work'. For example, Florence Nightingale, who is often considered the founder of contemporary nursing, promoted nursing as a 'woman's job'. Nightingale advocated that the moral traits of a 'good nurse' are identical to those found in a 'good woman' (Gamarnikow, 1978: 98). She naturalised nursing for women by associating nursing tasks with mothering tasks and also subordinated nursing to medicine, which was considered a masculine occupation. A health care publication from Nightingale's era states:

> Nursing is distinctly women's work ... Women are peculiarly fitted for the onerous task of patiently and skilfully caring for the patient in faithful obedience to the physician's orders. Ability to care for the helpless is woman's distinctive nature. Nursing is mothering. Grownup folks when very sick are all babies.
> (*Hospital*, 8 July 1905, p. 237 cited in Gamarnikow, 1978: 110)

It was not only Nightingale who depicted nursing in this way. Advocating for women's participation in the public realm, Cecile Matheson (1908) (cited in Walton, 1975) argued that nursing fulfils women's maternal urges. In the *Journal of Education* Matheson commented:

> the middle aged worker who is without home ties of her own tends to grow weary of life and to seek to crush maternal emotions that seem to exist to give her pain ... It is probably the innate craving for human interest that leads so many to take up teaching and nursing.
> (Cited in Walton, 1975: 82)

These connections that were made between nursing and mothering in nursing's early years helped to establish nursing as feminine. The proclamations made by Nightingale and others, as well as Nightingale's reforms, firmly associated nursing with nurturing and caring practices and mostly excluded men from the occupation. Under Nightingale's reforms the few men who were employed in the field were confined to asylum nursing as it was anticipated that this would be an area where their (assumed) superior physical strength would be most useful for restraining patients. Interestingly, and counter to normative education practice, this gendered division of labour was also supported by the provision of inferior psychiatric education to the male nurses. The female nurses received education that was superior in both quality and quantity (Evans, 2004; 323). This feminisation of this occupation was a classed process. According to Walton nursing 'in the early nineteenth century represented little more than a specialised form of charring, certainly not an occupation for ladies. However, by the middle of the century the situation was changing and nursing was becoming more respectable' (Walton, 1975: 13–14). The motivation for establishing nursing as a 'woman's occupation' was to provide respectable single women an income. Nursing was a job for respectable 'women of bourgeois and *petite bourgeois* origins who were forced, by adverse circumstances such as the lack or death of a husband or the lack of an inheritance, to earn their own living' (Gamarnikow, 1978: 111), and in the nineteenth century nursing evolved to 'an occupation for middle-class girls' (Miers, 2000: 75–6). The feminisation of this occupation was therefore driven by the needs of a particular class group.

Nursing was also open to '*respectable* working-class women' who were recruited 'to exert control over their own class'; it was open to respectable working-class women who wished to put a floor in their circumstances or gain some mobility. However, these women needed to commit to becoming more respectable and all nurses were required to learn to dress their hair in particular styles, wear their uniform in a particular manner, keep their gloves impeccably clean and adhere to indefectible hygiene at all times (indeed, stocking and glove checks continued in nursing until the 1960s). In this way, all nurses, but particularly working-class nurses, were required to govern their bodies 'and with this discipline came the authority to govern and regulate the patients – the poor – in their care' (Nelson, 2001: 31). Working-class women 'of good character' were therefore rewarded with social mobility for their commitment and service to nursing and this was an essential element of Nightingale's reforms (Nelson, 2001: 30). Yet, nursing was considered 'a *vocation* for middle-class women and a *job* for women of the [respectable] working classes' (Miers, 2000: 72). Therefore a hierarchy was generated to reinforce the class positions of workers.

Nursing was so feminised that women were responsible for the management of the occupation (Marsland, Robinson and Murrells, 1996: 232). However, traditionally, it was only a certain type of woman who became a senior nurse. According to Miers in the nursing tradition 'the "higher class" of women were eventually established as the guardians and the educators of the lower class nursing recruits'. Miers states that management was particularly dominated by the middle class because, while matrons and sisters did not tend to earn enough to be independent, 'nursing leadership became an occupation for "distressed gentle women", middle-class ladies who needed to earn their own living' (Miers, 2000: 38).

In contemporary Australia and the UK the feminisation of nursing continues: over 90 per cent of nurses are women (Pudney and Shields, 2000: 803, ANF, 2011: 2). Nursing also continues to be associated with caring, and the emotional skills required for nursing are naturalised as feminine because the connection between caring, mothering and nursing, established by Nightingale, persists. This has had consequences for nurse training and the professionalisation of nursing. For example, Pam Smith's (1999) study of nursing education demonstrates that while the image of nurses as caring is prominent in recruiting literature and publicity, emotional skills are not adequately addressed in training programmes, and students tend to receive little support with dealing with their own emotions as well as the patient's emotions (cited in Sharma and Black, 2001: 928). In addition, nurses have fought for their work to be perceived as involving both 'caring about' (a sense of feeling affection) and 'caring for' (servicing a person's needs) (Ungerson, 1983: 31); as emotional work is commonly devalued, nurses have fought for nursing to be depicted as involving both love and labour so that their occupation might be given professional status.

Unfortunately, the feminisation of occupations often equates with poor remuneration and as with other feminised occupations contemporary nurses are underpaid – the Australian nurse earns $152.20 less than other full-time adult non-managerial employees (ABS, 2005b: 4) and in the UK the average nurse's salary is £27 234 while the average wage is £29 999 (Anon., 2007). Further, nurses do not tend to be employed in full-time work, which is another characteristic of women's employment. In 2008 almost half (47.9 per cent) of all Australian nurses worked part-time (AIHW, 2010) and similarly, in the UK around two-fifths of nurses work part-time (Mercer, Buchan and Chubb, 2010: 14).

What is more, as nursing has become a more socially acceptable occupation for men, men have assumed more of the field's management positions. Men occupy a disproportionate number of management positions in relation to their numbers in the field. Glover and Radcliffe (1998) argue that in Australia overall, despite the fact that men 'only make up 7% of the nursing workforce, they occupy more of the senior positions' than women (cited in Glover and Radcliffe, 1998: 13). Brown (1995) suggests that 'in NSW in 1992, where men held approximately 7.9% of all registered nursing positions, they held 19% of senior nursing administrative positions' (cited in Brown and Jones, 2004: 6). This trend seems to be even more pronounced in the UK where, despite making up only 9 per cent of the nursing population, men hold just over half of all of the top nursing positions (Wright, Frew and Hatcher: 102). Unfortunately then, men's success in the occupation means that women are now disadvantaged in obtaining management positions; it seems that the occupation may provide less opportunity for women than it did in the Nightingale era.

Nevertheless, nursing continues to be an occupation in which women can *anticipate* employment. The ABS states that in Australia in 2001 '84% of women aged 15–64 years with a Bachelor degree or higher in a nursing field (155,000 women) were in the labour force' (2005b: 6). This is 'much higher than the labour force participation of all women (69%)' (ABS, 2005b: 6). In addition, 'women with nursing qualifications also experienced lower unemployment rates compared with all women (1.2% and 6.3% respectively)' and it is thought that when nurses are unemployed, it is largely due to family responsibilities (ABS, 2005b: 6).

### Enrolled nursing and the nursing hierarchy

There are a range of workers undertaking nursing so that there are several tiers to nursing in Australia and the UK and a clear hierarchy exists between nursing posts (at the bottom of this hierarchy there is a group that may be broadly termed personal or health care assistants, then there are enrolled nurses, registered nurses, nurse educators, nurse practitioners and nurse managers and nurse academics). My analysis will focus on the experiences of registered nurses (RNs) and enrolled nurses (ENs/SENs)[1] (although some of the registered nurses I interviewed have been promoted to nurse managers).

Very little research has been conducted on enrolled nurses and enrolled nursing students (McKenna et al., 2001: 5). However, it is known that enrolled nursing is an occupation which has become *increasingly* feminised in recent years. In Australia in 1996 93.9 per cent of all enrolled nurses were female whereas in 2001 94.5 per cent of all enrolled nurses were female (Meagher and Healy, 2005: 42). Moreover, according to McKenna et al. (2001: 5) 85.1 per cent of the students enrolled in the enrolled nursing courses in Australia's Technical and Further Education System (TAFE) in 2000 were female and 60 per cent were 30 years of age or older and therefore 'mature age' students.

Enrolled nursing graduates earn less than registered nurses: they earn between $34,000 and $38,000 per annum (TAFESA, 2006: 1). Enrolled nurses also earn less than those who are similarly skilled but are in masculinised occupations. For example, in 2004 female non-managerial enrolled nurses earned an average of $20.50 per hour while female non-managerial police persons earned an average of $26.20 per hour. Similarly, male non-managerial enrolled nurses earned an average of $20.10 per hour while male non-managerial police officers earned an average of $29.80 per hour (note too that women in these occupations earn less than men) (ABS, 2005a). However, once again, this is an occupation in which workers can expect high employment prospects.

Although enrolled nurses and registered nurses were hospital trained prior to the 1990s, they are now both predominantly trained in higher education institutions. Enrolled nurses are distinct from registered nurses as they undergo a shorter period of training in a further educa-tion institute rather than a university and they graduate at a lower skill level, they are therefore situated in a lower position in the field of educa-tion. In addition, according to the Australian Bureau of Statistics (ABS) the enrolled nurse '*assists registered nurses* [my emphasis], doctors and other health professionals in the provision of patient care in hospitals, nursing homes and other health care facilities' (2005b: 1). Enrolled nurses are therefore subordinate to registered nurses in the occupational hierarchy. Moreover, it must be noted that registered nurses are better paid than enrolled nurses and only registered nurses have access to the most senior positions in the nursing hierarchy such as an academic position or the position of Director of Nursing.

Dyer et al. (2008: 2032) argue that in health care the hierarchy (which these nursing posts are also a part of) is gendered and racial-ised. Those who are at the top of the hierarchy are male and white, while those who are at the bottom of the hierarchy are not. I would like to argue that this hierarchy, at least the nursing component, may be classed as well. As registered nursing is mostly populated by middle-class women, has a higher entry level and is paid more than these other posts, it may be the case that lower nursing posts are more heavily populated by working-class women. This is McDowell's (2009) observation as well. McDowell loosely defines those who are posted below registered nurses as 'care workers' and states:

> Care workers typically are middle-aged, working-class women, although their numbers are often swollen, especially, although not only in London, by migrant workers. ... Care work is low-status work and is often the last option for those with the most limited choices in the labour market.
>
> (McDowell, 2009: 170)

This hierarchy between different levels of health care workers is reiterated in everyday work interactions and activities. Enrolled nurses and personal or health care assistants most frequently submit to the demands of other workers, an emphasis is 'placed on deference to those in authority, on not asking questions, and doing what one is told' (Dyer et al., 2008: 2032). In addition, the lower down on the health care hierarchy an individual is, the more 'dirty work', body care they engage in (such as dealing with bodily smells, bodily fluid and heavy lifting (McDowell, 2009). Social distance is therefore created between middle-class and working-class employees in nursing and health care occupations more generally.

## Social work

Like nursing, historically, social work was constructed as a 'woman's profession'. Brown (1986) argues that there are two reasons for this. Firstly, this is because social work actually 'arose out of the efforts of women' to transfer some of their caring labour out of the private sphere and into the public arena (Brown, 1986: 223) (although social work is different to nursing in that in nursing women were moving into a profession where men were already established (Walton, 1975: 14)). In its early years those who advocated for social work to be considered women's work, largely did so as part of a broader campaign for women to have access to the higher education and paid employment; 'Every new employment for women was a blow struck in the struggle for emancipation, so that social work was a small part of a much larger clash to establish women as full participating members of the community' (Walton, 1975: 81).

Secondly, Brown (1986: 223) suggests that social work was constructed as a woman's profession because care-taking was and is seen as a feminine competence. Social work was depicted as nurturing work and therefore related to female roles the family (Walton, 1975: 257). Indeed, social work was even seen to stand in for mothering. Social work was seen as 'providing substitute experience for single women unable to marry, or married without children' (Walton, 1975: 257). These observations suggest that similar processes were at work in creating both social work and nursing as feminine.

Social work is also a classed occupation. British advocates for education like Emily Davies argued that unpaid and paid social work might be an appropriate avenue for educated women of a certain class.

In her book, *The Higher Education of Women*, Davies (1866: 77–8, cited in Walton, 1975; 17) argued:

Unpaid, work such as the management of hospitals, workhouses, prisons and reformatories and charitable societies, naturally devolves upon the leisurely classes and offers a field in which cultivated women may fitly labour. And the moment they enter such work, or attempt in any way to alleviate the sufferings of the poor, they find that a strong, clear head is as necessary as a warm heart.

In its early years, social workers were, for the most part, women with 'independent means' and the 'daughters or wives of small businessmen or men in the professions, comfortably off with a modest household' engaging in voluntary work (Walton, 1975; 18). Furthermore, social workers have often appeared to pursue middle-class objectives. For example, both Nell Musgrove (2004) and Mark Peel (2004) argue that the early practices of social workers in the Victorian welfare services consisted of moral middle-class interventions into the morality of the working class (cited in Mendes, 2005: 124). Walton (1975: 41) argues that in the UK moral welfare, particularly welfare work for the unmarried mother and child was important in the development of social work. Moreover, Richard Kennedy (1995) suggests that social work in Australia originated 'as a social measure to stave off political demands from the organised working class' (cited in Mendes, 2005: 125); it therefore served to limit struggle between the classes and create social distance between them. This occupation might therefore be characterised like nursing in that it is an occupation for middle-class women. However, it departs from nursing in that its *objective* was to reinstate the position of the working-class more generally.

Despite its feminisation, men did play some part in the development of social work. Walton (1975: 81) argues that most social work organisations were created by men or in conjunction with men and points out that women could not have entered the public realm without the support of the husbands and fathers that they were dependent upon. Furthermore, from very early on, men occupied senior positions. For example while the British Federation of Social Work council was largely made up of women, the first chairman was Mr H. E. Norman, a male probation officer (Walton, 1975; 154–5). In addition, there has always been a division of labour within social work:

the forms of social work where men predominated – probation, NSPCC, School Board Officers, duly authorised officer, relieving officers – all carried strong elements of authority and control. Thus, whilst it was possible for men to be motivated to social work, they tended to hold positions which mirrored family roles of authority, discipline and management.

(Walton, 1975: 258)

What is more, the areas of social work that have been predominantly populated by men, such as probation work, were the first to achieve the establishment of a universal service and decent salaries (Walton, 1975: 156).

These gendered and classed trends continue. In his 2004 study, Lewis (2004: 399) found that female social workers in Australia still tend to identify as middle class. Social work also continues to be female dominated. In Australia the proportion of women in social work is actually increasing – in 1976, 64 per cent of social workers were women and in 1991 this figure had increased to 78 per cent (Martin, 1996: 31). In 1996 the proportion of women in social work increased again – to 79.6 per cent; and in 2001 social work appeared to be even further feminised – 81.1 per cent of social workers were women (Meagher and Healy, 2005: 42). In the UK this is also the case. Malcolm Smyth (1996) survey found that in the UK approximately two-thirds of qualified social workers are women (cited in Christie, 1998: 493) and this proportion has probably increased – according to Perry and Cree (2003: 376) the number of male applicants to social work training have steadily declined since at least 1993.

Further, gender stratification appears to exist within contemporary social work just as it does in nursing; while women may numerically dominate this field, they do not necessarily hold the most powerful positions. According to Brown (1986: 225) exact figures on gender differences in social work management in Australia are not available and Martin (1996) also suggests that it is difficult to measure numbers in management via census data. However, it is known that men dominate the senior positions in Australia, and in the UK women only make up 7 per cent of the directors of social service departments (Howe, 1985: 21). Lewis (2004: 398) states that a pattern exists where 'men seek management positions and women are more likely to seek out clinical roles'. Moreover, when women do enter leadership positions, they earn lower salaries than their male counterparts (Brown, 1986: 225).

There are a range of posts that carry out social work besides social workers (for example, community welfare workers, youth workers and counsellors). This book explores the experiences of community welfare workers as well as social work practitioners (some of whom have been promoted to management and academia). These social service jobs are organised according to a hierarchy, largely informed by education, so that professional social workers occupy a more prestigious position in the social service industry than community welfare workers (social workers are trained in universities while community workers are not). Hence, in both the health care and social service industries, higher education may influence a worker's career and class trajectory.

### Nursing and social work as semi-professions?

As a side point I would also like to note that although both nursing and social work are respectable, middle-class occupations, they are also often labelled 'semi-professions' rather than professions and both occupations continue to campaign for more money and status. Social work and nursing have engaged in what Witz (1992: 64) calls 'professional projects':

> [S]trategies of occupational closure which seek to establish a mono-
> poly over the provision of skills and competencies in a market for
> services. They consist of courses of collective action which take
> the form of occupational closure strategies *and* which employ
> distinctive tactical means in pursuit of the strategic aim or goal of
> closure.
>
> (Sharma and Black, 2001: 914)

Labelling these occupations as 'middle class' or as appropriate for respectable women was one of these strategies, with limited success. This strategy's failure is perhaps because gender seems to dominate class in the making of professions so that men's occupations are primarily viewed as professions while women's are not. Various authors have commented on how the struggle for professional status for these occupations is less about skill and more about gender. For example, McDowell comments:

> Nursing is what was once termed a semi-profession (Etzioni 1969):
> the condescension in the label 'semi' associated with the dominance
> of women in occupations so categorized (Hearn 1982). ... Clearly
> these are demanding professions, based on sets of specialist skills
> and are usually graduate-only entry, but their reliance on a predomi-
> nantly female labour force reduces their status.
>
> (McDowell, 2009: 162)

This commonality between nursing and social work, as well as the similarities between their histories, cultures and demographics suggest that these occupations might also belong to the same field. Elsewhere (Huppatz, 2009), I have also suggested that the workers in both occupations exhibit similar dispositions, occupy similar positions and take part in similar struggles and so perhaps are components of a 'paid caring field'. This will be examined further in the analysis chapters.

## Exotic dancing

Exotic dancing is a term for stripping, lap dancing, table dancing and pole dancing. Throughout this book I use the terms stripping and exotic dancing interchangeably. Katherine Frank defines exotic dancing as

> a form of adult entertainment involving varying states of nudity, physical contact and constellations of erotic and personal services such as talk, fantasy and companionship. Strippers may perform on stages or perform individualized dances for customers.
>
> (Frank, 2007: 502)

Therefore, exotic dancing can involve a high level of physical contact but it also often involves a high level of verbal interaction with customers and emotional sensitivity to their needs. In addition, it requires that workers' bodies conform to an aesthetic that is both feminine and sexy.

Exotic dancing is often defined as sex work. Indeed, exotic dancing involves the provision of a sexualised service and exotic dancing and prostitution sometimes overlap. However, exotic dancing might also be described as 'service work'. IBISWorld (an industry-based commercial research company) locates the sexual service economy with wholesale and retail (Shulman, 2011: 30) and Siobhan Brooks (2010: 6) describes exotic dancing as a 'desire industry' in much the same was as she describes retail work: both these types of jobs 'operate on ideas of desire and attractiveness' just as fashion jobs, modeling and acting do. In other words, these jobs all demand a certain aesthetic.

Of course, the exotic dancing industry is a feminised industry. Gregor Gall (2007: 71) suggests that between 90 and 95 per cent of sex workers are women. However, in its beginnings, all exotic dancers were women. Exotic dancing originated in the US (Bindel, 2004: 14) and was derived from burlesque. In the US in the 1930s burlesque 'strippers and teasers' began to undress to pasties and a G-string (Shteir, 2004: 80) and this marked the beginning of exotic dancing. However, it was not until the 1960s, when burlesque theatres could no longer compete with the growing pornographic industry, that stripping became as explicit as it is today with an emphasis on 'close-up nude or semi-nude performance' (Prince-Glynn, 2010: 32) and exotic dance clubs began to open. At this point the occupation also opened up to men; and in 1978, after always being an entirely female occupation, some men, like the Chippendales, began to strip as well (Smith, 2002: 70).

Interestingly, as with social work and nursing, exotic dancing has a classed history too. In the later nineteenth and early twentieth century, as burlesque performers' performances became more sexually aggressive, burlesque fell out of favour with the middle class as the representations of femininity became too distant from respectable middle-class femininity (Prince-Glynn, 2010: 30). Therefore, while striptease in all its incarnations has always tended to be an occupation where working-class women 'could overcome their working-class origins and make it', from this point it predominantly catered for working-class audiences too (Prince-Glynn, 2010: 30).

Although the exotic dancing industry has a well-recorded history in the US, the history of striptease in the UK has not been documented in any detail (Hubbard, 2008: 6). It is known that London's Windmill theatre pioneered burlesque in the 1930s (although dancers were always stationary while naked) and later, after the 1968 repeal of the Lord Chamberlain's ban on striptease, Raymond's Revuebar in Soho, began to offer more risqué shows including fully nude dancing (Hubbard, 2008: 6). At this time stripping also started to appear in the East End at public houses. However, the first strip club in its modern form, providing '"intimate" forms of interaction between (female) dancers and (male) clientele where dancers "straddled" the seated customer' did not appear in the UK until 1995 when the Canadian chain *For Your Eyes Only* opened a club in outer London (Hubbard, 2008: 6). Even less is known about the culture and history of Australian striptease. The first strip club, the *Staccato* was opened by Abe Saffron in Kings Cross, Sydney in 1960 (Saffron, 2008) but there were no strip clubs in Melbourne until 1992 (Tyler et al., 2010).

Nevertheless, in both Australia and the UK, this industry has experienced rapid growth since the 1990s. According to Bindel (2004: 14) lap dancing has been described as 'the fastest growing area in Britain's sex industry and in the leisure industry in general'. There are now approximately 150 legally operating clubs in the UK (Bindel, 2004: 6), and Strip Clubs Australia, an online strip club directory, lists 48 registered clubs in Australia (Strip Clubs Australia, 2011) (however, in both countries there may be even more clubs, it is difficult to know exact numbers as some operate without a licence or do not define themselves as lap dancing clubs (Bindel, 2004: 6)).

In Australia, dancers and strippers earn approximately 17 per cent of the sex industry's revenue (Shulman, 2011: 7). In his IBIS report, Shulman (2011: 7–8) finds that growth in this industry in recent years is partly due to the rise in high-end gentleman's clubs in urban centres and the growth of large franchised brands like Spearmint Rhino (which has 2700 employees and 6000 entertainers globally) (Shulman, 2011: 26). This industry is also becoming increasingly normalised and its advertising is now permitted on billboards and television. However, 'while there has been some rise in consumer acceptance of sexual services, the industry still has a negative image, largely due to the moral, health and safety issues associated with it' (Shulman, 2011: 12).

In Australia there are between 15,000 and 20,000 sex workers employed at any one time (Shulman, 2011: 13). However, the nature of the sex industry is seasonal and many workers are not employed fulltime. For these reasons the average salary in the industry is only about $27000 despite opportunities to earn high hourly wages. Workers are most motivated to join the sex industry in times of unemployment and under-employment and many workers are only employed in the industry for a few years to achieve a financial target (Shulman, 2011: 5–30). Therefore, sex industry jobs appear to function as back up jobs or 'last resorts'.

Gall (2007: 71) comments, 'sex work and sex workers represent a form of "atypical" work, whereby working patterns and forms of work organisation are non-standard, and there is often no employer so that no employment contract exists, implied or otherwise'. Within Australia, working conditions for exotic dancing vary between states and territories. However, within the Australian state of Victoria and in the UK, as with most other parts of the world, dancers 'are self employed and therefore have no employment rights. They pay a fee to work in the clubs. The private dance is the only legitimate way for the dancers to make money' (Bindel, 2004: 7). Exotic dancers are therefore vulnerable employees, and for this reason, in both countries, the industry has recently unionised. In 2001 exotic dancers were asked to joined the GMB (Britian's General Union) and in 2002 a union titled 'Striptease Artists of Australia' (SAA) was formed to represent exotic dancers (and in 2006 it gained an industry-wide bargaining award through the Australian Industrial Relations Commission). However, union commitment is sporadic and according to Bindel (2004: 8) in the UK the majority of club owners are opposed to dancers joining the British union. This very recent push for unionisation in this industry is interesting because it shows that this type of work is becoming less deviant but it also shows that these workers have very different concerns to the concerns of nurses and social workers who secured unionisation long ago and now seek to enhance their autonomy and professionalisation. As with nursing and social work, men hold the top positions in the sex industry and strip clubs are mostly owned and operated by men. In addition, while most exotic dancers are women, their clients are mostly men. Shulman has found that 'sexual services are principally provided to adult males (between the ages of 18 to 55 years), comprising 84% of industry revenue, and people in households with higher than average income' (2001: 15). Clients are frequently married men, bucks parties, business associates and tourists (Shulman, 2011). This industry is therefore still typified by specific gender interactions: women do exotic dance while men consume it. While Shulman (2011) predicts that over the next 5 years there is likely to be an increase in female clients for the sex industry, he suggests that it is probable that women will always be a niche segment of the market.

## Hairdressing

Like exotic dancing, hairdressing is an industry that has a fairly short history in the UK and Australia. Before the Second World War many women did not have their hair cut at all and for the affluent hairdressing was performed by domestic servants. However, after the Second World War hairdressing became a significant part of the British economy. Margaret Attwood and Frances Hatton (1983: 116) suggest that there are two ways in which women were impacted by the world wars and that these impacts triggered the production of the hairdressing industry. First, women necessarily entered the paid work force due to the absence of men and therefore started to change their appearance and wear shorter hair. Second, paid work also became more accessible for working-class women and so fewer domestic servants were available for hairdressing services from this period onward.

Hence, significant changes in gender and class roles contributed to the birth of the hairdressing industry. As women began to enter the public realm 'hairdressing services became both a market for women to spend their earnings and a new career for predominantly working-class women' (Attwood and Hatton, 1983: 116). Hairdressing was also an industry where women could become legitimate entrepreneurs. However, as the beauty industry expanded in the first 20 years of the twentieth century, it was taken over by men. Further, 'the establishment of professional organisations and the striving for a new professional respectability within the industry was initiated by the men newly associated with the beauty business, and had the effect of marginalising the small salon and the small scale business woman' (Black, 2004: 31). This is why the names that were associated with hairdressing throughout the 1950s and 1960s (such as Raymonde, Vidal Sassoon and Xavier Wenger) and are now 'folk heroes' are all male (Attwood and Hatton, 1983: 117).

Nevertheless, although men dominate the top ranks, hairdressing is still a feminised occupation and salons tend to be feminised spaces. In the UK 90 per cent of hairdressers and beauty workers are female (Habia, 2008) and in Australia 91 per cent of hairdressers are female (ABS, 2005a). Furthermore, not only are the workers in salons mostly women, they are also encouraged to be as feminine as possible – well groomed, pretty and sympathetic to their customers' needs and feelings. In addition, the customers are also mostly women and the product is, more often than not, a more feminised self – a hairstyle that falls in line with dominant conceptions of feminine beauty. As Jo Lindsay states, 'hairdressers simultaneously adopt their own version of gender and create versions of gender for their clients' (2004: 261). Even the reading material given to customers tends to be women's magazines like *Vogue* and *Grazia*, which mostly deal with issues of fashion and beauty.

Hall, Hockney and Robinson define hairdressing as 'a skilled manual job associated with creativity and aesthetics' (2007: 540). Hairdressing is therefore very different from nursing and social work in that it is a 'trade' and is never referred to as a profession. In addition, researchers have found that it is predominantly working-class girls and women who attended public schools who staff the hairdressing industry (Attwood and Hatton, 1983; Lindsay, 2004). Moreover, perhaps because it is both feminised and working class, in both the UK and Australia hairdressing is poorly paid. Attwood and Hatton (1983: 116) suggest that hairdressing's historical ties to domestic servitude also contributes to its low status. Nevertheless, as hairdressing is skilled and morally uncompromising it is perhaps considered more respectable than a job in the sex industry.

Hairdressing continues to be considered *appropriate* for working-class women: 'Possibly beauty therapy is – as secretarial work used to be – a kind of "feminine" work seen as a realistic aspiration for the working-class girl yet not *infra dig* for the middle class girl' (Sharma and Black, 2001: 916). In addition, it continues to be *imagined* as working class.

As Debra Gimlin (1996: 510) observes there is an archetypal image of hairdressers that circulates in popular culture:

> Cultural images of the hairdresser abound, so much so that she has very nearly become a social type. One can imagine the hairstylist played by Dolly Parton in *Steel Magnolias*, a frosted, painted, girdled icon of fabricated femininity who dispenses not only permanents and hair dye but also small-town gossip, marital advice, and tissues for her customers tears. Or one might imagine the ridiculously coiffed 'beauty school dropout' from *Grease*, whose overzealous commitment to avant-garde beauty culture alienated her from other (less adamant) devotees of adornment. We find frequent-and rarely flattering-images of women who immerse themselves in beauty culture and attempt to bring the culture's practices and belief system to the lay masses.
>
> (Gimlin, 1996: 510)

This archetype, I might add, is working-class. She occupies suburban salons and embodies working-class femininity; she does not quite get high-fashion femininity 'right'.

The customers of hairdressing salons are also class subjects and hairdressing produces a classed aesthetic. Historically, only the affluent had access to hairdressing services so that in Victorian England a groomed appearance marked out an individual's class position. Black states: 'What beauty preparations did for white middle-class Victorians then was to mark class and racial boundaries, as well as divisions within classes. They also developed an image of delicate and natural femininity which Bhavani (1997) argues still operates today' (2004: 35). Only white middle-class and upper-class women could afford to maintain a polished appearance, while other women engaged in domestic labour. Today, hairdressing, like other forms of service work, continues to play a part in the management of class distinction (Gimlin, 1996; Lindsay, 2004). As Lindsay states, 'hairdressing plays an important role in self-representation for most people. Hairdressers are ubiquitous service workers involved in the ongoing creation of gender and class with their clients' (2004: 259). Moreover, hair treatments, cuts and blow-dries are also leisure-times practice for the affluent, visits to the hairdresser are not only about regular grooming or self-maintenance but also pampering, self-indulgence and relaxation.

The working conditions in the hairdressing industry are not ideal. As I mentioned earlier, hairdressers tend to be poorly paid and they earn considerably less than those who are similarly skilled. For example, in 2004 in Australia female hairdressers earned an average of $14.60 per hour whereas female mechanical engineering tradespersons earned an average of $21 per hour, similarly male hairdressers earned an average of $14.00 per hour while male mechanical engineering tradespersons earned an average of $23.90 per hour (ABS, 2005a). In fact, in both Australia and the UK it is the lowest paid of all the trades and one of the lowest paid occupations more generally (Lindsay, 2004: 260; Stewart, 2011). Hairdressing is also physically demanding. As Lindsay states, 'Physically, hairdressers are on their feet most of the day, managing the danger of chemicals, scissors and other equipment. There are few rest breaks and a constant turnover of clients (Eayrs 1993)' (2004: 264).

However, the hairdressing industry is heterogeneous and 'there is a hierarchy between salons, which flows through to the nature of the hairdressing work that is undertaken' (Lindsay, 2004: 264). While at the bottom end there are shopping mall and suburban salons in which haircuts are quick and cheap and hairdressers are very poorly paid, 'at the top end are the "funky" salons that participate in hairdressing competitions and service famous clients in the media, fashion and music industries' (Lindsay, 2004: 264), where hairdressing is expected to be creative and haircuts take at least an hour. This hierarchy in positions and workplaces indicates that there is potential for success and profit-making in this industry. However, perhaps due in part to the poor working conditions as well as the need for hairdressers to embody a fashionable, attractive aesthetic, this is an industry for the youthful so that in both the UK and Australia workers tend to be under 35 years of age (DEEWR, 2009: 3).

## Conclusions

This chapter has demonstrated that although they may not be fields in themselves, nursing, social work, exotic dancing and hairdressing have specific cultures and these cultures have been sustained throughout time. The historical, cultural, structural, economic and demographic 'profiles' of the occupations presented in this chapter also indicate they are all feminised and that they are all classed. Therefore, although men do sometimes work in these occupation and workers in each occupation are not always similarly classed, workers do appear to share a social proximity so that there appears to be 'a central hub' for each occupational group, a mean gendered and classed position around which workers swarm (Atkinson, 2009: 907–8). The consistency of feminisation in particular indicates that the workers may exhibit some similar dispositions, may in some ways be similarly positioned, and may sometimes take part in similar struggles across all of these occupational groups. Moreover, the significance of gender for these occupations means that they may be social arenas in which gender is an asset; they may be social spaces where gender capital operates, and the profiles point to the kind of gendered embodiments that may be valuable in these social spaces.

However, these occupations are of course different and, in particular, they are differentiated by class: nursing and social work appear to be middle-class jobs and exotic dancing and hairdressing appear to be working-class jobs. In addition, professional status has not been granted to exotic dancing or hairdressing and both occupations are plagued by particularly poor working conditions. It might also be added that exotic dancing and hairdressing also differ from nursing and social work in that they are commercial enterprises and are less directly associated with 'caring' even though, as they are also service jobs, they do appear to involve emotion work. Moreover bodily aesthetics appear to be more important for working in exotic dancing and hairdressing (although historically bodily aesthetics were significant for nursing too). Hence, although all of these occupations may be fruitful spaces to explore the intersections of gender and class and the operation of gender capital, some of the gender capitals that circulate in exotic dancing and hairdressing may be very different to those which circulate in nursing and social work.

# 4
# Collecting and Interpreting Work-Life Stories

The previous chapter provided an outline of the cultures, histories and demographics of the four occupations that I focus upon in this book. This chapter moves on to outline some of the processes involved in collecting and interpreting work-life stories from those who participate in these occupations. Essentially then, this is a methodology chapter, it details how and from which standpoint I carried out research on these occupations. Significantly, it details how I operationalised Bourdieusian and feminist Bourdieusian concepts. Although methodology sections of papers and books can sometimes be dry, this discussion is an important inclusion, as, as Skeggs (1997: 17) argues: 'To ignore questions of methodology is to assume that knowledge comes from nowhere allowing knowledge makers to abdicate responsibility for their productions and representations'. The first section of this chapter will introduce the subjects of the study; the workers who kindly shared their stories with me. Then, in the second section of the chapter I will outline how I identified class identities as well as gender identities in the research and finally, in the last section I will discuss my standpoint on eliciting narratives and how I framed the research questions.

## The participants and their occupations

As the previous chapter discussed, the feminised occupations of nursing, social work, exotic dancing and hairdressing were chosen as areas of study because they are all gendered. These occupations are also similar in that they may be loosely defined as service jobs and although they clearly involve different tasks, because they are associated with femininity, there are commonalities in the nature of the labour that is involved. This may mean that similar gender stories might be expressed by workers involved in these different occupations and, importantly for the focus of this book, *gender capitals* might be required for and valued in these occupations. Yet these occupations also differ in terms of their histories, cultures, economic remuneration, working conditions, the training required and the status and respectability they are afforded. And although occupation cannot stand in for class, it is linked to class, so that workers may be divided in terms of their class experiences.

A range of workers were interviewed for this study. Fifty-three workers were interviewed in total including 25 nurses, 20 social workers, 5 exotic dancers, 3 hairdressers. Most of the participants were women, only five of the participants were men (four nurses and one hairdresser). However, this is to be expected when dealing with feminised occupations.

The participants in this study largely self-identified as working class or middle class and as coming from working-class or middle-class backgrounds and these identities loosely correlated with their occupation or their position within their occupation. For example, almost all of the exotic dancers and hairdressers identified as working class and as coming from working-class backgrounds. In contrast, the nurses and social workers largely identified as middle class and as coming from middle-class backgrounds. However, the further education students who were training for junior or less prestigious positions within this cohort also tended to identify as working class and as coming from working-class backgrounds. As was discussed in the previous chapter, these differences in class identifications within and between these occupations are not unusual and reflect the status and class cultures of the occupations. In this way, the data supports Bourdieu's (1987: 4) aforementioned proposition that occupation 'remains a good and economic indicator of position in social space' (cited in Atkinson, 2009: 903); that clouds of people roughly correspond to occupations. However, as occupation still cannot stand in for class, this was found to be a tendency rather than a rule.

## Locating class

Before I progress to the analysis I would also like to briefly comment on the process that was involved in locating the participants' class backgrounds for this study. This component of class-based research is often glossed over in methods sections of academic papers and texts and yet it plays a very large part in determining the sort of data researchers collect. This book aims to understand some of the processes of class-making; to explore how class (and gender) are articulated, made and reproduced in occupations. This means that I do not approach class as a category, as I stated in Chapter 2, Bourdieu argued that classes cannot be determined 'a priori' (Weininger, 2005: 85). For Bourdieu, the boundaries of class can only be understood in terms of social practice via empirical enquiry. As I discussed in Chapter 2, for Bourdieu classes are relational – people are clustered in social space and their class is defined in terms of the distance between them and the direction in which they are heading (Atkinson, 2009: 903). Class is a therefore a dynamic concept.

However, I needed a starting point in order to understand the class processes particular workers are involved in and the class processes involved in the making of feminised work environments. I needed some idea of individuals' class histories so that I could understand where the workers had come from in relation to where they are going. I also needed to have some understanding of the resources they might draw upon or have drawn upon in their movements through social space, including their movements into and within these occupations. In addition, it was important that I understood how workers see their own identities, for as Skeggs (1997: 2) argues, agents also play a role in their own class identification; people are 'not just ciphers from which subject positions can be read-off; rather, they are active in producing the meaning of the positions they (refuse to, reluctantly or willingly) inhabit' (Skeggs, 1997: 2). Therefore, in order to initiate the exploration of individuals' classed habituses and the practices they inform as well as the capital individuals hold, the workers who participated in this study were asked to self-identify their class backgrounds and class positions. This, I reasoned, does give some indication of their histories, their experiences of class movement and their attitudes to class and class membership. Furthermore, this self-assessment was provided in conjunction with details on individuals' class capital and lifestyles: information about education, area of residence and parents' occupations.

These self-identified class positions and backgrounds for the most part were consistent (their self-identified class backgrounds and positions as well as their class capitals and lifestyle all unambiguously pointed to either a working-class or middle-class identity and position). However, sometimes they did not 'match up' or conflicted with the workers' other class indicators, such as their dress or mannerisms. Several of the workers stated that they came from middle-class backgrounds, without there being any evidence to support this and even though they also mentioned that they did not have much economic capital growing up and that their parents participated in blue collar jobs. For example, Jacquie stated that she comes from a middle-class background even though her mother is a dental nurse and her father is a labourer. Similarly, Tracy stated that her class background is *middle class maybe* even though her mother is a childcare worker and her father is a truck driver. Abigail also claimed that hers is a middle-class background when she was initially asked to reflect on this issue, however, later in the interview she stated that she comes from a *fairly poor farming background*.

Some of these inconsistencies might indicate class mobility (and a number of workers did discuss experiences of mobility) but they also demonstrate the muddy nature of class-identification. The inconsistencies I discovered may demonstrate that the boundaries of class are often experienced as uncertain, particularly when one is seeking mobility. Reay (1997: 228) suggests that for the mobile working class this is a 'class landscape of "maybe" and "perhaps" where personal history shapes current consciousness and where there are none of the certainties of conventional middle-class horizons'. Inconsistencies also serve to highlight another significant factor about working-class culture – as Skeggs (1997) and Reay (1997) have also discovered working-class people are often reluctant to identify as working class, simply because the working class is seen to be of a lesser value than the middle class. As Reay states, 'to own an identity as "working-class" is, among other things, to accept one's social inferiority (Neckel, 1996)' (1997: 228). Furthermore, as I will argue below, the research interview is a performance and by reiterating that theirs is a middle-class history workers may be attempting to produce a stable sense of middle-class identity that would assist in their movement or transition, for it is possible that, in this way, a person's disposition may impact their position. Finally, these inconsistencies perhaps indicate a decline in awareness of class identity, a phenomenon that has been outlined in detail by individualization theorists (such as Ulrich Beck 2007). They also might provide evidence of the often unconscious and misrecognised nature of the habitus, which also makes using this singular method of identifying class histories and positions less than ideal (as opposed to a multiple method, like Bourdieu's multiple correspondence analysis, that can be used in large-scale studies).

It was also interesting to note that some of the participants were quite certain of their histories as well as their current class positions and offered this information readily. Therefore, some of the workers put much conscious thought into their class dispositions and positions. This reflexivity was often displayed by the self-identified working-class participants. For example, Eliza commented: *The area that I grew up in is a working class area and all my friends and family were working class and I was proud to be working class.* In addition, the working-class participants in the study who work in nursing and social work (two middle-class jobs), were very quick to discuss their working-classness, indicating that this reflexivity is perhaps enabled by a lack of 'fit' between their class habituses and the workplace culture. For example, Janet stated: *I don't believe I'm middle class (laughs)!*

For others, particularly those who self-identified as middle-class, and as coming from middle-class backgrounds, class history and position were difficult topics to broach. For example, Alice had difficulty answering these types of questions because class was not a concern for her. Alice stated: *Um ... I don't really look at that ... but I'd say we sit in the middle ... yeah.* Similarly, Helen stated that she had trouble thinking about class because her parents *would never have spoken class* with her:

> I don't know, I suppose my father had a very responsible job he was probably. ... I don't know what would you say middle class? I've never thought about it. They're not class people if you know what I mean. They were certainly on all the invitation lists to all the cocktail parties and goodness knows what that went on in Canberra in those days, so the diplomatic circuit they were involved in, but they would never have spoken class with us.

Again, this response may be a symptom of a general decline in class awareness. However, I would like to suggest that this lack of reflexivity is also a privilege of the dominant – the dominant do not have to reflect on their privileged position or on the inequalities that result from it. The middle class is a powerful group in both English and Australian societies and as a dominant group they are constructed as the norm and adjacent to the (working-class) other.

These inconsistent and troublesome class identifications make the analysis of class identities and histories a difficult task. Furthermore, as I have discussed, categorising does not sit well with a dynamic understanding of class identity. Nevertheless, it was essential to gain some sort of picture of the participants' class histories as a starting point for analysing the narratives; in order to explore the participants' habituses, their movements, experiences of social distance, the practices they inform and the capitals they hold. Self-identification combined with other indicators, also respected the participants ability to locate themselves as class subjects.

## Locating gender

Within my enquiry I also wished to determine the participants' genders so that I could determine whether this cohort of workers are female like most other workers in feminised jobs. In addition, I wanted to draw connections between gendered identities and gendered practices, movements and capitals as well as classed dispositions, practices, movements and capitals.

How did I know that I was dealing with subjects of a particular gender? As with class, I asked the participants to identify their gender. In this way, again, I am subject to the participants interpretations. However, I also read gender off their bodies through physicality, mannerism and dress (for, as Bourdieu (2001: 103) argues, gender is 'inscribed in bodies and in a universe from which they derive their strength'). Hence, the participants' self-identifications as well as my own 'readings' of their bodies informed a starting point for analysing the worker's gendered experiences.

Interestingly, it seemed that, unlike class, identifying their own gender was straightforward for all of the participants. Perhaps this is because many seemed to link it to their sex, which they see as an unambiguous, biological reality. This is not surprising as it is this 'taken for grantedness' of gender that allows a feminist interpretation of it as a primary form of social stratification; as I mentioned in Chapter 2, McCall (1992: 844) states that this allows for an interpretation of gender as a primary, yet elusive social force which appears as natural and universal. However, this is not to say that the workers I spoke with do not resist or deviate from the normative gender behaviours and embodiments that are associated with their identified gender or that their gender is never misconstrued.

As I stated in Chapter Two unlike Bourdieu, I follow the feminist tradition that sees gender as 'inherently ambiguous, contradictory and unstable' (Skeggs, 2004: 24). This impacted the way in which I approached the data. For example, I looked for diversion from norms as well as consistencies in gender practice. I also move beyond Bourdieu and follow the approaches of West and Zimmerman (1987) and Judith Butler in that I see dispositions as not only inscribed but also accomplished or performed in interactions and looked for ways that gender performances may operate as assets or capitals. What is more, I recognised that not all women have equal access to valuable femininity. This is because hegemonic femininity is classed ('... it was a category produced from a struggle to impose a model of an ideal bourgeois femininity (Walkerdine, 1989)' (Skeggs, 2002: 20)) and raced. It is a femininity that is produced in certain economic and cultural conditions, in particular power relations and in the interest of particular groups (Skeggs, 2002: 20). Similarly, I acknowledged that hegemonic masculinity may not be available to all men (Connell, 1991). In sum, in analysing the data I was mindful that, while some ways of doing gender are subordinate and others are dominant, men and women live out gender in different ways and that multiple femininities and masculinities exist.

## Narratives

The interviews I carried out with workers elicited personal narratives. I have named the participants' narratives 'work-life stories' for two reasons. First, they convey significant detail about their career 'choices', work experiences and pathways as well as the relationship between gender, class and occupation. Second, their narratives often departed from work issues but even their work stories revealed much more than just work activities – they revealed something about the ways in which these individuals *live* gender and class, are limited by gender and class, engage in gendered and classed relations and mobilise gendered and classed assets – they are life stories.

I chose personal narrative as a resource for data collection as personal narrative '… is situated, embodied and material – stories of the body told through the body which make cultural conflict concrete and accessible' (Langellier, 2003: 447). Moreover, the personal narrative is an important means for providing marginalised groups with a political voice for expressing their identities and experiences (Langellier, 2003: 446). It has the 'transformative power to assert self definitions about who matters and what matters: the existence, worth and vitality of a person or group as meanings not otherwise available.' (Langellier, 2003: 454) and so is an invaluable research tool for a feminist project that seeks to provide insight into gendered and classed experiences.

Using narrative is to assume that there are no 'dualisms between self and society. Material social conditions, discourses, and narrative practices interweave to shape the self and its many identities' (Lincoln and Denzin, 2003: 240). Hence, to value narrative is to approach the interview process from a particular theoretical standpoint – it is to understand that general social processes can only be known through their embodiments. As Chase states:

> Understanding general social processes requires a focus on their embodiment in actual practices, that is, in actual narratives. In other

words, life stories themselves embody what we need to study: the relation between this instance of social action (this particular life story) and the social world that the narrator shares with others; the ways in which the culture marks, shapes, and/or constrains this narrative; and the ways in which this narrator makes use of cultural resources and struggles with cultural constraints.

(2003: 290)

The narrative approach, with its focus on embodiment, is therefore compatible with Bourdieu's conceptual approach, particularly his focus on habitus and dispositions.

In addition, Langellier (2003) also argues that the personal narrative (including the interview narrative) might be viewed as both performance and performative. The personal narrative is 'a site where the social is articulated' and 'structured' and is also a site where the social is 'struggled over' (Langellier, 2003: 446). Narrative provides the researcher with direct access to the practices that constitute change.

## Eliciting the work-life stories

Bourdieu's theoretical insights as well as Bourdieusian-feminist insights directed this research. In a sense I was testing a theoretical understanding of the social world, broadly outlined in Chapter 2. Questions put to the interviewees aimed to yield some understanding of workers' gendered and classed dispositions, struggles, differences and distances (Atkinson, 2009: 908). In addition, they were designed to ascertain whether certain bodies and dispositions worked as assets within particular occupations. Therefore, while the aim of the empirical study was to collect narratives, these were to be 'structured' narratives, in that I was interested in covering quite specific 'topics' and so I designed an interview schedule that related to these topics.

Within the interviews I sought to enquire first and foremost about capital. As stated in Chapter 2 this research necessarily moves beyond Bourdieu in that, not only did I study the relationship between men and capital, I also investigated the relationship between women and capital. I took up Lovell's (2000: 22) suggestion, and elicited narratives which indicate the 'capitals' possessed by women, the composition of that capital, and the extent to which its deployment is controlled by women.

Within this study I also took up the feminist proposal that gendered capital may exist (Lovell, 2000 and McCall, 1992). In particular, I responded to the suggestion put forward by Skeggs (2004) and Lovell

(2000) that uniquely *feminine* forms of capital might be wielded by women. I suspected that as feminised work is where women tend to have a good 'feel for the game', and is a social space where particular feminine bodies and dispositions are valorised, feminised work may also be an area in which feminine capital operates. Moreover, in line with my earlier findings (Huppatz, 2009), I examined the operation of *female* capital. Female capital is the gender advantage that is derived from being perceived to have a female (but not necessarily feminine) body. Female capital may be an asset if stakeholders are interested in maintaining female domination of these occupations when hiring and promoting.

In *Masculine Domination* Bourdieu (2001: 77) commented 'it has often been observed that women fulfil a cathartic, quasi-therapeutic function in regulating men's emotional lives, calming their anger, helping them accept the injustices and difficulties of life'. Emotional competence may therefore often feature in, and be valued as, an aspect of feminine identities. Bourdieu (1998: 68) also commented on emotional labour stating that 'this work falls more particularly to women, who are responsible for maintaining relationships'. Therefore, in seeking information on the feminine dispositions that are valued in these occupations, a particular attribute I enquired about was emotional competence.

Arlie Hochschild (1983), who pioneered research on emotional labour, argues that emotional labour involves the emotions of the person who is the object of the labour as well as the emotions of the worker. She discusses the relationship that this work has to the labour market, stating that 'emotional labour is sold for a wage and therefore has an *exchange value*' (Hochschild, 1983: 7). Furthermore, Hochschild comments that jobs that call for emotional labour have three characteristics in common:

> First, they require face-to-face or voice-to-voice contact with the public. Second, they require the worker to produce an emotional state in another person – gratitude or fear, for example. Third, they allow the employer, through training and supervision, to exercise a degree of control over the emotional activities of employees.
>
> (1983: 147)

Emotional labour is now a significant aspect of economies in rich nations because as Leidner (1993) shows, a growing numbers of jobs, especially at the end of the lower end of the labour market, 'involve 'interactive work' in which the service and the service provider are inseparable' (cited in McDowell, 2000: 205). McDowell (1997) has also shown how emotional labour is increasingly a feature of professional occupations. Moreover, a number of other sociological theorists talk about the feminisation of emotional labour (for example see Hochschild, 1983; McDowell, 2009; Sharma and Black, 2001) and, as I discussed in Chapter 2, Reay (2004), with reference to her study on mothers' involvement in their children's schooling, argues that women wield emotional capital. Therefore, I wanted to build on these understandings of emotional labour and explore whether emotional skills (particularly caring and nurturance) operate as feminine cultural assets within these types of feminised work. Accordingly, I spoke with workers about their interactions with clients and patients and their experiences of, and attitudes to, this labour.

Another, related issue I wished to explore was the significance of bodily aesthetics for these occupations. It has been argued that aesthetic labour is an integral part of service industries (see for example Witz, Warhurst and Nickson, 2003). Aesthetic labor is similar to emotional labor in that it 'refers to aspects of jobs that require workers to enact particular emotional states in order to manipulate clients or customers. The two concepts share a focus on the embodied characteristics of workers' (Williams and Connell, 2010: 352). However, aesthetic labour is less about performing a role in a particular employment context as is the case for emotional labour and more about 'expressing deep-seated dispositions. In other words, when hiring, employers are looking for workers who already embody a particular *habitues* (Williams and Connell, 2010: 352). Embodied dispositions of femininity, masculinity, class and race as well as social capital, cultural capital and age are commodified (Pettinger, 2005: 461). Employers are looking for individuals who bear particular social positions and capitals upon their bodies and this habitus is used by employers for competitive advantage. The bodies and clothes of many workers 'form a "network of signs" to communicate meanings to shop customers and where labour is aestheticized' (Pettinger, 2005: 468). This is a process that may be visible in hairdressing and exotic dancing, and, as I discussed in Chapter 2, it was once present in nursing as well and may have some residual impact. For example McDowell suggests that hairdressing 'not only relies on feminine attributes such as tact, sensitivity and compassion, but it also works on the female body and its adornment' (2009: 188). Hence, I examined whether this means that bodily dispositions are also wielded as capital by employees in gaining entry to, and succeeding in certain occupations. In particular, I tried to ascertain whether a feminine bodily aesthetic operates as feminine bodily capital in feminised jobs.

Embodiments of class may also be valuable in the service sector. In particular, high-end retail work requires a high-fashion aesthetic as well as middle to upper-class modes of speaking and deportment. As Bourdieu (1984: 206) observed, many occupations that involve 'presentation and representation' require the abolishment of 'all traces of heterodox taste' and a 'dignity of conduct and correctness of manners' which implies 'a refusal to give way to vulgarity or facility'. As Black (2004: 115) suggests this means that questions need to be asked about employees' class and ethnic backgrounds – we need to enquire as to who has the necessary capitals for service employment and how easily they may be acquired. I therefore explored whether middle- and upper-class modes of femininity, particularly middle and upper-class feminine bodily aesthetics operate as capital and, in contrast, whether working-class feminine bodily aesthetics are detrimental in these occupations. In addition, Bourdieu commented that

> The interest the different classes have in self-presentation, the attention they devote to it, their awareness of the profits it gives and the investment of time, effort, sacrifice and care which they actually put into it are proportionate to the chances of material or symbolic profit that they can reasonably expect from it.
>
> (1984: 202)

And for this reason working-class women, 'are less aware than all others of the 'market' value of beauty and much less inclined to invest time and effort, sacrifices and money in sacrificing their bodies'. I therefore examined whether different workers from different classes are differently invested in bodily capital.

Researchers have speculated that the significance of emotions and corporeality for feminised jobs may have had an impact on men's participation. For example, McDowell argues that traditional masculinity might be unwelcome in feminised workplaces:

> In a profession such as nursing which is so heavily imbued with notions about emotional labour, men might be expected to be at a disadvantage as the oppositional construction of rationality and emotions which maps into a male/female divide seems to construct them as out of place.
>
> (2009: 176)

I therefore examined whether masculine capital is as profitable as feminine capital within feminised occupations.

In addition, as appearance and emotion is now so important for feminised work, particularly service work, many men might find that it does not fit with their habituses and also that participation contradicts the doxic system of gender relations; 'For many young men the attitudes and servility demanded in the performance of these menial service occupations are regarded as unmasculine and demeaning' (McDowell, 2000; 205). As feminised work seems to be so closely associated with femininity men also risk stigma and various other forms of symbolic violence if they become involved. McDowell (2009: 176) states that men:

'...find their identity and/or their sexuality challenged if they adopt what are constructed as feminine attitudes and behaviours at work, whether in the classroom or the hospital ward (Heikes 1992; Isaac and Poole 1996; Evans 1997; Alvesson 1998)'.

Nevertheless, some men do participate in feminised work and so I examined whether men who participate in feminised occupations feel a sense of 'fit' in these spaces. I also looked at men's experiences of gender capital and how masculinised and feminised capital may be utilised by both men and women. In doing so, since men do appear to hold a disproportionate number of senior positions in feminised work, I explored how men also develop a good 'feel for the game' in a feminised social space and the relationship between masculine and feminine, male and female capitals. I rationalised that this may be a space where men demonstrate feminine embodiments or take part in feminine performances in order to gain entrance into or 'fit' the social space, but it also may be a space like many others in that masculine and male capitals may trump feminine and female capitals.

Further, I explored whether or not feminine dispositions are used as capital to improve or change class positions. Due to the fact that there exists a large amount of low paid and 'low skilled' feminised jobs so that 'the demand for caring is rising while the demand for "masculine physicality" is falling' (Lovell, 2000: 25) women from lower classes may utilise shared meanings about their feminine dispositions to improve their social and economic positions. This means that women's decisions to enter feminised jobs may not predominantly be an operation of gender differentiation and distinction, women may take part in 'feminine' performances in order to obtain more stable or powerful economic positions. What is more, men from poorer backgrounds may be more likely to transgress gender boundaries in order to 'get ahead'. Or perhaps, as Bourdieu (1984: 382–3) suggests, it is only middle-class men who are willing to embrace femininity. Hence, I looked at the ways in which gender 'passing' may assist in the transgression of class lines, or may be consistent with class practice.

In addition, I examined whether class may be used as capital to change feminine positions. I examined whether those who occupy more prestigious positions are from higher socio-economic groups. Further, I explored whether this type of class history endows agents with a better 'feel for the game' – whether, (as Lovell (2000: 18) suggests), certain class positionings enable the crossing of gender positionings. I hoped that by examining this intersection of class and gender this research might be able to provide a partial answer to one question asked of Bourdieu: how 'do some women manage to develop a good feel for "games from which they are excluded by virtue of their sex?"' (Lovell, 2000: 14). Moreover, I anticipated that the findings may provide evidence either for or against Bourdieu's (1984: 382–3) claim that gender differentiation is less obvious in the higher classes.

This last focus was also examined from a different angle: while class may assist in improving a feminine position, a feminine disposition may also limit class advantage. According to Skeggs, (1997: 10) femininity may only be used as capital in a very limited way: in a 'tactical' manner (this is why women's autonomy tends to be achieved in 'hybrid' forms). Drawing from de Certeau's (1988) definitions of these concepts, Skeggs (1997: 10) explains that while strategies have an institutional positioning, tactics may merely manipulate constraints in the absence of power. Hence, in correspondence with this observation, I examined whether gender interacts with class in a way that nullifies its institutional backing and limits its strategic uses. In other words, I explored whether when intersected with gender, class too, is only a tactical (as opposed to strategic) benefit. Alternatively, McCall (1992: 846) suggests, women's gendered capital may never be profitable because gender is an, 'asymmetrical category of perception'. As Moi (1991: 1036) argues, gender capital may not exist – femininity and femaleness may be 'negative symbolic capital' (s). Or, as Adkins and Lury (1999), argue women's feminine dispositions may not be as profitable as men's because they are perceived as natural (see also Adkins, 2005). Again, masculinity and maleness may trump femininity and femaleness.

I also explored a further (and more recent) suggestion made by Skeggs (2004) – that the definition of capital may be more useful if it were to be opened up and extended beyond high culture so that other cultural practices and dispositions may also be seen as resources which can be exchanged across fields. I looked at whether femininities other than upper middle-class femininity might be exchanged to workers' advantage. In particular, it examined whether working-class femininity is ever valuable, particularly in hairdressing and exotic dancing, which, as was explained previously, are considered working-class careers.

Finally, I looked for acts of resistance and examined the struggles of workers. I looked at whether workers struggle over the value of forms of capital within these occupations, as well as whether they contest the gendered and classed meanings assigned to their occupations. Therefore, I explored the state of play within feminised jobs. In addition, I examined whether individual women 'choose' to pursue feminised work as an outcome of symbolic violence, or a fulfilment of gender norms or whether they are motivated by something else altogether. I also examined whether, since they risk stigmatisation through their participation, a feminised career choice is difficult for men and I questioned participants about their parents', partners' and friends' attitudes to their career choices to look for experiences of social struggle and symbolic violence.

## Conclusions

This chapter explained how I went about studying, class, gender the intersections of class and gender, and  gender capital in four occupations. This chapter explained how I identified the gender and class identities of the workers who shared their stories with me, outlined a rationale for my method of data collection and I also described in some detail the specific issues I explored when eliciting the work-life stories. In particular, I described how the issues I examined within the interview process were informed by Bourdieu's understandings of class, gender and occupation but also feminist re-workings of Bourdieu and other feminist work on emotional and aesthetic labour.

The following four chapters present the findings of this research – they examine worker's experiences of gender, class and gender capital in nursing, social work, exotic dancing and hairdressing.

# Part II
# Locating Gender Capital at Work: Four Case Studies

# 5
# Nursing

As I discussed in Chapter 3, nursing is a particularly feminised occupation, it is feminised both numerically and culturally. For this reason the majority of the nurses I spoke with identified as female and much of my discussion in this chapter pertains to women's experiences. In particular, the occupational choice process seems to follow a similar pattern for many of the female nurses I spoke with, a pattern that contrasted with the occupational choice experiences of the male nurses I spoke with. For many of the female nurses, irrespective of their class background, this occupational choice fulfilled social expectations, a desire to participate in caring activities, or was made under the threat of some kind of social sanction. So I would like to start this chapter by discussing how, for women, the choice to pursue nursing often falls in line with, and reaffirms, the gendered doxic order – how 'doing nursing' is 'doing femininity'. The second part of the chapter will look at the role of class in nurse's career choices and how motivations to enter the occupation appear to not only be different for men and women but also for working-class women and middle-class women. In the final section I will look at the role of gender capital in workers' entrance into and movement within this occupation and discuss women's and men's experiences of femininity as a limited asset.

## Gender stories

### The importance of caring
Most nurses work in clinical practice and so work 'to promote, good health, prevent illness, and provide care for the ill, disabled and dying' (ANF, 2011: 2). Nursing is therefore seen as 'caring work' because it

involves the care-taking of human bodies. It is not surprising then that the majority of the female nurses discussed nursing in terms of fulfilling a desire to 'help', 'care' or 'nurture'. For example, Louise stated: *It's about helping people; it's about making a difference, and the ability to do that at different levels, and different spheres of influence.* Interestingly, however, rather than emphasising the technical aspects to this caring labour (such as administering medication and setting IVs), most of the female nurses stated that they were drawn to this job because they desired to take part in 'caring about' (a sense of feeling affection) rather than 'caring for' (servicing a person's needs) (Ungerson, 1983: 31). In other words, they emphasised the significance of emotional aspects to care work.

In contrast, this element of nursing work was not emphasised as appealing by the male nurses. This is perhaps an outcome of the cultural alignment that is made between caring and femininity. Caring, particularly 'caring about', is linked to the feminine practice of mothering which is associated with women's bodies (an association that is reiterated in Garminkow's (1978) quote in Chapter 3 and, as I will discuss later in the chapter, was articulated by the female nurses) so that 'caring about' is a feminine practice of distinction. This means that the female nurses' gendered habitus' may be directing and creating consistency in their career choices; their habitus' appear to be working beneath consciousness, shaping feminine, caring aspirations that are in line with a doxic system that differentiates masculinity and femininity.

### Fit between dispositions and positions

What is more, because of the association between mothering and caring, simply by participating in caring work, all of these women, regardless of their class histories, are, at least in their working lives, doing femininity well. And for many of the female nurses this appears to provide pleasure and a sense of 'fit'. For example, Abigail stated: *I just kind of fitted into nursing.* Similarly, Alice stated that she experiences a 'fit' because nursing is a place where her gender not only has a position but also an *impact* and that this fit is something that male nurses do not tend to experience:

> *Well, I think you look for jobs ... where your gender has an impact. And I mean, even now there's more male nurses but I still think that that they find it harder to fit in you know, where you've got a female dominated profession.*

Therefore there is congruency between feminine dispositions and the occupational space so that 'fit' is experienced. As Bourdieu (2001: 57) argues 'the essentially social logic of what is called "vocation" has the effect of producing ... kinds of harmonious encounters between dispositions and position'. Women carry out feminised work felicitously (in both senses of the word). However, class may also play a role in this 'fit'. While caring motivations were discussed by most of the women, a desire to participate in 'caring about' or emotional caring was most often emphasised in the narratives of middle-class women. This will be discussed in more detail later in the chapter.

## Maternal worlds

The habitus often shapes feminine practices beneath consciousness so that they have continuity with the practices of other women. Bourdieu (2001: 26) argued that young girls often remain in the 'maternal world' while boys generally depart from it, which means that females live 'in a kind of continuity with their mothers'. Bourdieu (2001: 95) argued that principles of 'vision and division' are 'transmitted from body to body', for example from mother to daughter, 'below the level of consciousness and discourse, to a large extent they are beyond the grip of conscious control'.

This process of bodily transmission is illustrated by the experiences of a number of the female nurses. Whether they cited caring as a primary motivator or not, many of the female nurses are carrying on a familial occupational tradition in that they are working or studying in the same field as their mothers so it is therefore likely that their mothers influenced their occupational choices. Mavis stated with pride that her mother had been awarded the French Legion of Honour for her nursing work in the civil war, and mentioned that *growing up with stories from my mother* had a significant influence on her career choice. Similarly, Mary commented:

> *I suppose my mother had a big influence on it (Mary's choice), she used to tell the most amazing stories of her nursing days and during the war, especially all the fun they used to have, the laughs ... they must've had some terrible times but we'd only hear the funny stories. And she was rather a brilliant raconteur, she is, she's still alive, and I guess growing up you sort of thought how romantic of her and so I didn't think of anything else.*

Interestingly, both Mary and Mavis identify as middle class, so there is both gender and class continuity in their choices. The continuity between their choices and their mothers' gives insight into how the occupation continues to be middle class and also how a family's class position is reaffirmed through intergenerational career choices.

For some of the other women, nursing is not necessarily a family tradition but their career choice is nevertheless akin to their parents' choices in that nursing is a highly gendered occupation. The majority of the parents of these female nurses work or worked in highly gendered areas (for example, their mothers worked in areas such as child care, homemaking, and secretarial work and fathers worked in areas such as electrical work, engineering and building).

Although her mother was not a nurse, Abigail acknowledged the importance of continuity in gender roles for her family:

> *but certainly back in the 70s and 80s when I was looking at career choices that (gender) was a big thing then. And coming from a very traditional background with a mother and a father who had traditional farming roles, that was important.*

It seems then that there is a continuity that exists between the work lives of many of the female nurses and the work lives of their parents. Gendered occupational traditions within families might therefore reproduce differentiated gendered (and classed) identities and relationships and illustrate the workings of the habitus.

In addition, it might be noted that many of these women have formed romantic partnerships with other individuals who work in highly gendered areas. The majority of their partners are male and tend to work in masculinised areas such as policing, car mechanics or bank management, and the female nurses who are partnered with women are partnered with other female nurses. So, these women live in particularly gendered worlds; they *and* their significant others take part in a gendered division of labour in the public realm.

Nevertheless, these gendered processes do not always occur seamlessly, for example, they are not evident in the male nurses' stories and nursing was not necessarily a preference for all of the women.

### Limited choice

Despite their discussions of choice, many of the older female nurses stated that they entered nursing because there were simply very limited options for women when they finished their schooling. For many of the older nurses, nursing was the best option from a choice of two or three occupations. Indeed, when they entered the field, many of the women were unaware that other occupations existed for women. As Louise stated:

*Well, at the time women did two or three things, they became a secretary, they went teaching or they did nursing basically. I'm talking early 1960s.*

Some of the female nurses also articulated their choice as an outcome of socialisation and a component of the wider division of labour. For example, Tracy also made reference to her upbringing. When asked if her femininity influenced her career choice Tracy replied:

*Yeah, I'd say so, yeah.*

*Q: Why?*

*Tracy: Because I think that caring … being caring is brought into you as a child if you are female. In my background you should be caring, you should be nurturing and all that sort of thing.*

Here, again, a gendered disposition has been encouraged by this nurse's family. A gendered habitus and participation in a gendered practice of distinction appears to be the outcome of socialisation.

Therefore, despite nursing bringing pleasure and reward, limits have been set on the practices of many of the women, particularly the older nurses. The doxic system order of gender differentiation has determined what is for, and what is not for them.

Some of the women's comments presented thus far demonstrate how women can also be complicit in the limitation of their practice. As Colleen commented, *I always thought nursing was the thing to do, the female thing to do.* In this way, women limit their actions so that they deny themselves access to activities and areas of social life that they are already denied access to. Colleen took part in this process again when she discussed her original career aspiration:

*Well, I always wanted to do medicine but we couldn't afford to do medicine. And my father died when I was six … and it was a pretty rough road for mum after that. But I could have gone via Legacy, but I always thought that was accepting charity so I didn't want to accept charity so I did nursing instead. I thought it was the next best thing and in hindsight I think it was probably better for me. Because medicine is about curing and nursing is about caring. That's my concept.*

Colleen therefore reiterated the doxic order within her narrative – she reinstated the symbolic system which aligns women with caring and men with curing. Colleen naturalised caring for women so that to be denied the opportunity to cure is not to miss out – it is to find a better 'fit', for a feminine habitus. As a side point, her narrative also shows how she may have transgressed gender norms if her family had more economic capital – demonstrating that adherence to gender norms is sometimes necessitated by class position rather than some kind of biological fulfilment.

Some of the women are very conscious of the role that societal expectations played in their career choice. For example, when asked if her femininity played a role in her occupational choice Louise replied:

*Yeah, I think it probably did, yeah.*

*Q: Why?*

*Louise: Because it was a socially accepted thing; that's what women did.*

These examples show that these women's actions are often in line with the gender order and at times the nurses are quite reflexive about this. This reflexivity demonstrates a momentary break with doxa, yet this action does not necessarily equate with sustained dispositional change and their continued participation maintains the gender order.

### Ordinary gender relations

Due to the strong alignment between nursing and femininity, symbolic violence was evident in the choice process for many of the female nurses. For example, many of the older women resorted to nursing because their parents did not view university as gender-appropriate. Mary stated:

*Although, I guess if I had any regrets it's the fact that I didn't really look into options, other options, it was just assumed that ... yeah ... I don't know, I suppose my parents probably thought it was a waste of time a girl going to university because she'd get married. You know they're in their nineties, and this is ... their attitudes are very outdated now.*

Others chose a gender-appropriate path because their parents failed to give them any career guidance. This was Julie's experience:

*I would think most probably because my mother believed that women got married and had children and therefore was completely unable to provide me with any guidance as to what I should do, and therefore I think my feeling is I fell into it (nursing) because they were unable to provide guidance, my school really didn't provide terribly much even though I was at a private boarding school.*

Jane, who is not a nurse but a social worker, observed how her guidance counsellor recommended nursing to young women regardless of their skills:

*But then again I remember with the career counsellor ... when people couldn't decide what they wanted to do she always suggested nursing. That could've played a role for a lot of people.*

Gendered symbolic violence has therefore impacted some female nurses' work choices. As Bourdieu suggests, this violence not only operates upon bodies but *through* them; it is through communications with others (men *and* women) that many of the female nurses made their occupational choices. These communications reinforced the doxic system, so that nursing sometimes truly became the *only* choice for many of them. This type of violence appears to be an 'everyday' occurrence that is carried out by individual agents (men and women), and often in the institutional contexts of the family and school. It seems then that symbolic violence is an 'extraordinarily ordinary social relation' (Bourdieu, 2001: 2).

Men are not immune to this violence either. Linda discussed her family's support for her gendered work role and the symbolic violence that is inflicted upon men who pursue feminised work:

*... we're slowly getting more males in but it's still ... you know most guys are still considered to be pansies or ... For those that are university trained it's becoming more accepted, but they've still got the stigma attached to them. There's something wrong with them because they don't want to do labour intensive work or something else. I could probably say that I don't think my dad or my mum would be happy if one of my brothers wanted to become a nurse, they would be like 'what are you doing?' So I suppose it was acceptable of me ... my career choice was acceptable to them.*

Linda's observations about the stigma attached to male participation in nursing are correct: all of the male nurses' discussed the social sanctions that they have experienced as a result of their occupational choices. Kimmel (2001: 273) has argued that masculinity, 'historically and developmentally ... [has been] the flight from women' (cited in Robinson, Hall and Hockey, 2011: 36). For this reason, the male nurses' family and friends did not always understand their choices to take up a job that is aligned with the feminine. For example, Russell talked about how his friends and family disapproved of his choice to pursue nursing:

> *My father couldn't understand and was completely against it: 'why would you want to go and wipe arses for a living?' I had another friend who said a similar thing, my mother wasn't too keen ... it hurt a bit ... even a couple of gay friends ... most people couldn't understand it ... I was bit defensive ... I justified my position, explained it in economic terms.*

Unlike the female nurses, Russell could not discuss his career choice in terms of 'fit'; social disapproval meant that Russell needed to justify his choice to pursue nursing by emphasising the economic benefits of this work. In addition, Russell experienced the most disapproval from his father who emphasised the 'dirty' elements of this work and cannot imagine why he would want to be associated with it. Russell's occupation choice has therefore particularly strained his relationships with his father, who sees construction work as more gender-appropriate: *Dad was proud of me as a construction worker, because it was macho enough.*

For Russell's Dad construction work is the appropriate social space for a man, as it provides masculine work positions and it affirms and possibly enhances masculine dispositions, whereas nursing does not. These experiences may further explain why the male nurses, in contrast to the female nurses, did not emphasise caring motivations for entering the occupation: even though they do feminised work they may still want to maintain some distance from the feminine and limit the symbolic violence they are subject to.

In addition, because these men are not perceived to be doing hegemonic masculinity well, it is assumed that, because of the close relationship between gender and sexuality, they do not do hegemonic sexuality well either:

> *There is also this negative meaning given to nursing that you are either gay or promiscuous depending on your sex.*
>
> (*Ned*)

Stan found that this assumption was so frequent that he started wearing a wedding band just to avoid the social stigma:

> *... they'd ask the question, 'oh, are you gay then?' and then when I put the wedding ring on, it stopped all that. They wouldn't ask the question. It was easy. It made it easy.*

These experiences also show how tightly normative masculinity is bound with heterosexuality. Judith Butler (1990) has explained how gender and sexuality are constituted relationally: '... that is how heterosexuality "makes sense" against its "other", homosexuality, and how this underpins distinctions between male and female and masculine and feminine' (cited in Robinson, Hall and Hockey, 2011: 36). Male participation in nursing unsettles this gender order and this is why male nurses' gender and sexuality are questioned and their social status is undermined. These experiences also give some insight into why many men avoid nursing.

These findings are not unusual for research on feminised work; they have also been mirrored in other studies. For example, Sargent (2000: 413), in his discussion of male school teachers reflects on the difficulties that men experience trying to conform to 'the proscriptions and prescriptions regarding masculinity' and also discusses how men in feminised occupations are viewed suspiciously for going against masculine norms (cited in Robinson, Hall and Hockey, 2011: 38). Similarly, Lupton (2000) 'argues that working in a female dominated occupation often does not allow men to easily confirm hegemonic masculinity, either within the workplace or their lives more broadly, and men risk being both feminized and stigmatized as a result' (cited in Robinson, Hall and Hockey, 2011: 37). There are therefore considerable obstacles to opening up feminised work to men.

### Divergent dispositions

Although nursing is a normative occupation for women the occupational choice process did not conform to a gendered script for all of the female nurses, either. Some of the women did not choose to pursue nursing because they wholly identify with its feminine symbolism, for some, nursing was an 'afterthought'. For instance, particular circumstances and a love for biology influenced Christine's career choice. Christine stated:

> *I guess probably when I chose to do my nursing it was more favourable circumstance rather than making a big a decision that I have always wanted to do nursing. I wasn't a person who grew up and always wanted to do nursing, but I definitely loved biology, I know that sounds quite strange, and definitely once I started the training I realised that it was a good fit with me.*

Christine's narrative not only demonstrates how women can be differently motivated, her love for biology also suggests that nursing is not only constituted by caring. As will be discussed later in the chapter, while nursing is often chosen as an expression of femininity, sometimes women primarily see nursing as a money-making opportunity or as an occupation in which they may trade their gendered assets. In addition, the quote above suggests that it was only once Christine was in the occupational milieu that she experienced a sense of 'fit'. This highlights how sometimes occupational spaces *produce* a fit between dispositions and positions, so that individual's dispositions are impacted by the social environment. As was suggested in Chapter 2, not only do occupations attract certain classed and gendered dispositions, they sometimes also produce or enhance them as well.

### Performing caring

Whether they were motivated by a desire to care or not, some of the nurses also admitted that they experience difficulties in carrying out emotion work. For example, Colleen commented that sometimes when dealing with patients she does *not* care. This means that in order to carry out care work, her emotions need to be kept in check: *What I probably have to do at times is curb those instincts*. As Hochschild (1983) identifies, this is often an aspect of emotion work – workers need to control their emotions while they work on the emotions of others. However, Colleen's comment is interesting because it seems to run counter to many of the other nurses' experiences of caring as innate and natural and it suggests that sometimes 'caring about' must be worked at and performed. Colleen's narrative demonstrates that women do not always embody caring dispositions and feminine capital. As Adkins (2004: 207) argues, norms are never wholly embodied.

### Class stories

As I mentioned in the previous chapters, the nurses I interviewed are a mix of enrolled nursing students, registered nurses and nurse managers so they occupy different 'posts' in nursing. In keeping with the historical makeup of nursing, most are middle class, however, the posts also appear to be stratified by class. For instance, the enrolled nursing students tended to identify themselves as occupying working-class positions and coming from working-class backgrounds. This is not surprising as, as I discussed in Chapter 3, nurse assistants or enrolled nurses are subordinate to registered nurses and earn less than registered nurses. In addition, as I will discuss at greater length in the next chapter, further education is subordinate to university in the field of education and typically educates more working-class people.

In contrast, most of the registered nurses saw themselves as coming from middle-class or upper middle-class backgrounds. Strikingly, all of the managers, apart from one male manager who identified as coming from a working-class background, claimed to have come from middle-class backgrounds. This suggests that agents from middle-class backgrounds, particularly women, may have a better feel for 'the game' in this occupation (Bourdieu and Wacquant, 1992). As was discussed in Chapter 2, according to Bourdieu, each field may be likened to a game in which 'players' hold particular 'positions' and exhibit strategic orientations toward the game depending on the amount and type of 'tokens' they hold, that is, the volume and structure of their capital. The strategies of a player depend on the evolution of the volume and structure of their capital over time, on their social trajectory and habitus (Bourdieu and Wacquant, 1992: 99). Although nursing might not be a field in itself it does seem that middle-class women are advantaged in this social space; when it comes to entrance into this occupation, a middle-class habitus and the 'tokens' or capital acquisitions that tend to be enabled by a middle-class habitus (such as educational capital) are privileged.

### Middle-class motivations

As I mentioned earlier, the majority of the female nurses indicated that a desire to participate in caring labour was their primary motivation for pursuing nursing and this is perhaps due to the importance of caring, particularly 'caring about' or emotional care-taking, for the construction of feminine identities. However, the propensity to experience this motivation may also be reflective of the female nurses' common class background because the few working-class nurses who participated in this study were the exception to this rule – they did not tend to communicate a desire to take part in emotional care-taking.

This may be because a caring demeanour is an important component of middle-class femininity; Ungerson (1983: 165) comments that middle-class women tend to engage in emotion work that 'affirms, enhances, and celebrates the well-being and status of others'. It seems that for middle-class women caring assists in the constitution of the 'right' femininity. Indeed, as I discussed in Chapter 3, Florence Nightingale, the founder of modern nursing, asserted that a good nurse is simply a good woman (Gamarnikow, 1978). Nightingale therefore made a link between doing caring work and feminine respectability: doing gender well in itself provides respectability. Hence, caring holds both gendered and classed meanings for the middle class. Indeed, nursing may be a 'caring career' because it was established as an occupation for middle-class women.

Moreover, the classed meanings attributed to caring may be another reason why nursing is a source of mobility for working-class women, as Skeggs (1997) found in her study, working-class women can achieve moral superiority and therefore respectability through caring performances. On occasion, the self-identified middle-class women responded with confusion to questions concerning motivation so that their choices appeared to operate beneath consciousness. For instance, Harriet stated: *I just always wanted to be a nurse.* Cynthia stated that the desire to be a nurse started in childhood: *I don't know, it was just one of those things you always wanted to do when you were a kid, that's probably it, just something I always wanted to do.* It seems that there is such a tight fit between their class/gender habitus' and this occupation that neither Harriet nor Cynthia can articulate why they pursued it. Middle-class doxic assumptions have naturalised caring dispositions and paid professional caring positions for these women.

This of course, is how class habitus' work – the habitus generates aspirations and practices which are common to each particular class group so that they appear 'sensible' and 'reasonable' (Bourdieu, 1991: 79). There is therefore a dialectic relationship between dispositions of the habitus and positions within fields. The doxic order structures both mental life and social life so that both perceptions and social relations are based on hierarchical social divisions. What is more, this further demonstrates the middle-class nature of nursing – as these participants see nursing as the 'natural' place for them, they are identifying this occupation as middle class.

### Working-class motivations

As I stated previously, Gamarnikow (1978) argued that nursing has traditionally been a *job* rather than a vocation for working-class women and many of the working-class women certainly seemed to approach nursing as a means to an end. For example, one third of the enrolled nursing students stated that their career and study choice was motivated by the desire to earn more money. Tina stated:

> *I still remember the first day when we had orientation by the teacher and they asked the question 'what makes you like to do this course?' And I just said 'I just want to get a job and make some money and pay my mortgage' (laughs). It was really simple.*

In addition to economic rewards, for the majority of the working-class nurses, a desire for *stable employment* was or is a motivating factor in pursuing this career path. For example Melissa stated that she hopes that enrolled nursing will end a long period of unstable employment:

> *I guess it's got good career opportunities, good travel opportunities that will come with it and it's more of a stable career path. Because I've just been finding that every two years I've just been going from job to job so it's more of a stable career path. Especially considering I was still single ...*

Tina desires stable employment, more money and further choice:

> *I have been here (in Australia) nearly nine years including this year and I have tried many jobs. In the past few years most of the time I work for Chinese and Chinese boss are more concentrated on business and the money for employee is quite low and I started to think about 'why not try something a bit different?' and I have been told 'well, if you become a nurse you have plenty of choice'.*

For Tracy enrolled nursing is more stable and more profitable than the personal care work in which she was previously engaged:

> *... I worked in a nursing home part-time as well as working still in the beauty industry. But as a personal care worker you don't ... it's not very good money. And then what I did is I worked for a family, with just one lady and that was pretty good money but the only problem is when that lady passed away there's no income. So I needed some kind of security, so nursing I also see as a security thing, you know, everywhere they need nurses.*

These narratives suggest, as do Game and Pringle (1983: 101), that 'nursing is seen as a means of upward mobility for working-class women'. These findings are significant because they indicate that these women are driven by financial needs – they are not only, or even primarily, motivated by an innate desire to 'care', even though they are women. Rather, femininity is used tactically, to floor their economic circumstances (Skeggs, 1997: 102). As with the working-class participants in Skeggs' (1997: 102) study, these women are deploying femininity 'to halt losses, as a way of trying to generate some value'. They are attempting to stop their employment situation from becoming any worse.

The desire for employment that is 'stable' or 'secure' indicates that these workers are conscious of, and are responding to, a labour force which, in an age of globalisation, is increasingly transient and unpredictable. As Kelly and Furlong (2005: 207) point out, the labour forces in UK and Australian are becoming increasingly precarious. Not only are there rising unemployment rates, there are also groups of workers who 'rarely encounter unemployment yet fail to make in-roads to relatively secure sectors of the economy or to the types of unemployment that will equip them with transferable skills' (Furlong and Kelly, 2005: 213). Indeed, according to Beck's 'Brazilianisation thesis' '... unemployment rates are being achieved on the basis of increased insecurity, poverty and socio-economic polarisation with the dichotomy between unemployment and employment being less and less relevant' (Kelly and Furlong, 2005: 213). The casualisation and impermanence of the British and Australian workforces significantly impacts women (ACTU, 2004; Walby and Olsen, 2002). Moreover, casualisation rates are highest for low-paying industries which involve little training (Walby and Olsen, 2002). Hence this is a phenomenon that particularly impacts working-class women. The working lives for this particular stratum of women have become increasingly uncertain.

While these economic concerns were frequent in the narratives of the enrolled nursing students, economic interests did not feature strongly in the narratives of the women who occupy the other posts. This is perhaps due to the fact that the majority of the registered nurses and nurse managers are already in stable occupational positions (although stability of employment in this occupation does not translate into high wages). They are also working in an occupation that has fairly high employment rates (indeed this is the reason that many of the enrolled nurses are training to enter the field).

Having said this, there were notable exceptions to this tendency. Like the enrolled nursing students, a few of the more senior women also discussed economic motivations for their entry into nursing. Linda, a registered nurse from a working-class background, was also economically motivated in that she discussed the significance that a desire for a stable income played in her career choice:

*I suppose so, I suppose it did. You know a stable income as in I knew what was going to be coming in every fortnight. With my parents being farmers it used to be dependent on the weather. They couldn't actually say this is how much we're gonna ... is their base wage because it was all depending on things beyond their control.*

Similarly, when questioned about her career choice Abigail replied that she was motivated by *being paid to do training* (she made her career choice when a university education was not required). Abigail stated:

> When I first left high school having come from a fairly poor farming background, to get money was an important thing for me. I'd originally thought that I wanted to be a schoolteacher but because we didn't have money to get through college education and things like that, I had to think of things that could pay me at least so that I could get some savings and a lot of my friends from school went nursing, so basically back in ... what was it, probably 1976 or 1978, our choices predominantly for girls in our rural sort of school was either nursing or teaching, so.

Colleen, who is a manager, shared a similar story because her parents could not finance a university education:

> And the options other than university and doing something other than what was part-and-parcel of your family membership was teaching, nursing and I guess the priests – though that didn't come into my thought process at all because it was very masculine ... Teaching I would never have ever dreamed of doing, and I always thought nursing was the thing to do, the female thing to do.

Abigail and Colleen's stories are common among the older interview participants. As Mavis observed: ... *a lot of women, poor women, women in the country ... had no way to get out of the situation they were in, except* (by pursuing) *teaching or nursing or secretarial work* ... For these women, nursing was not only a gendered choice, it was clearly an economic choice; it was a means to an end for many respectable working-class women. Here class clearly intersects with gender to limit occupational choice.

Furthermore, all of the male nurses I spoke with stated that they 'fell' into nursing due to a lack of job opportunities in their previous occupations or their geographical locations which means that they also appear to be 'halting losses'. For example, Stan, a male, working-class nurse manager, stated that he initially entered the field because it was a significant step up, in terms of pay, reliability and status from factory work:

> I worked in a factory when I first finished school and then I had a friend who had tuberculosis and he said 'why don't you work in a hospital instead of a factory?' so then I became an orderly.

Nursing may therefore offer working-class men, who are willing to be associated with feminised work, the same protection it affords working-class women. What is more, as the nurse managers whose narratives were discussed in this last section appear to have come from working-class backgrounds, it again seems that nursing can be an avenue for class mobility.

Economic considerations were also significant for women who were forced to take on breadwinner positions for their families. The occupational pathways of several of the women from *both* working-class and middle-class backgrounds enabled an income when they separated or divorced from their partners. When asked if this career path had improved her financial situation Mavis stated:

> *It's a bit like the cart and the horse. What it has done is that ... when there was a point in my life where I was in very difficult financial situation it meant that I had a way of making money and a way of climbing out of a level of poverty. So yes it has.*

Similarly, when asked the same question Harriet stated: *But then my husband and I separated, so definitely. I guess though working shift work is what keeps it* (her income) *up there.* Feminised work therefore enables women an independence from men. It ensures that they are not impoverished without the income of a partner. In this way, although participating in paid caring labour is a normative activity for women, the income derived from it can enable an economic freedom that has not traditionally been afforded to women. Once again, femininity is used to 'halt losses' within women's lives (Skeggs, 1997: 102).

Other middle-class nurses did not talk about economic motivations but nonetheless discussed the economic benefits of their career pathway. For example, Christine appreciated the economic benefits of nursing because she is one of the few women from the higher posts who (like the enrolled nursing students) had experienced unskilled employment at some point. When asked whether nursing paid better than her previous career Christine stated:

> *Oh much better pay. I was in an unskilled position. I think that was one of my motivations for doing nursing, because you could still work forty hours a week and make terrible pay, be bored out of your mind: at least with nursing you were never bored, you're always busy. Everyone should have one of those jobs (laughs).*

However, economic gains and promotion only ranked moderately for the middle-class women. When economic gains or promotion appeared to be important to these women they tended to be thought of as something that would be achieved in relation to student wages (which is not a permanent or accurate measure of advantage); or in relation to dabbling in other less stable and economically rewarding occupation pursuits (for example one participant used to be a 'shop girl' and another used to be a visual artist); or assisted them when they separated or divorced or their partners could no longer provide the primary income. Hence these women appear to be class *repositories* in every sense of the word. For the most part they do not appear to be interested in high wages and the accumulation of further economic capital; they merely solidify and pass on family capital (Huppatz, 2010).

### Reconciling money and care

As caring and femininity are intimately tied so that caring holds significance for the construction and reproduction of feminine identities and is considered an appropriate and even 'natural' pastime for women, particularly for middle-class women, the few middle-class women who also expressed economic interests appeared to experience difficulty in reconciling their desire for money with their desire to care. For example, when asked about her motivation for pursuing nursing Samantha stated: *The truth? I wanted a job that I could make money and go travelling with. There was nothing benevolent or holistic about what I did ... or not holistic, but you know, wholesome.* Hence, despite breaking with her peers in terms of motivation, Samantha nevertheless positions herself with the caring discourse. She is defensive about having interests *other* that caring interests. The occupational social space, which is shaped by middle-class values, including the prioritisation of femininity and caring and the devaluation of economic interests (caring carries more moral weight if it is altruistic, and 'good women' are those who are selfless), continues to impact her cognitions and desires. Thus, Samantha only experiences a partial break with doxa.

### Ordinary class relations

The working-class women's parents did not always encourage them to pursue this middle-class occupation. This may be because their parents did not see these careers as a good 'fit' with the type of person they considered members of their family to be. This is the case for Tracy. Tracy did not self-identify as working class, but hers is an unclear history as she is one of the workers who had other class indicators which pointed to her having a working-class background (such as her parents occupations and her dress and mannerisms). Tracy commented on her parents' lack of support for her occupational choice:

> *They thought it was really bizarre, they were like 'really, really, are you sure you want to do that?' They were really down on it – **they didn't think I would be capable of handling the responsibility and everything of it.***
>
> *Q: What did they think would be more suitable for you?*
>
> *Tracy: Well actually, I was a beauty therapist and so they thought that was more my type of thing because it's beauty, fashion ... yeah. They think it's a lot more easier, and they don't think that I'll be able to cope with the pressure of nursing.*

Tracy's parents therefore prefer that Tracy remains in a trade instead of pursuing this middle-class profession. Tracy's parent's reaction to her career choice illustrates something about working-class culture. As Skeggs (1997: 11) states:

> Not being middle class is certainly valued in many working-class social groups. In fact careful monitoring for pretensions often takes place, evidenced though long-standing clichés, such as 'too big for your boots', 'full of airs and graces' or 'stepping out of line'. Clichés as Walkerdine and Lucey (1989) note have the useful purpose of reminding us who we are.

This is precisely what Tracy's parents are doing: they are reminding her of *who she is* and where she has come from. This is a way of establishing working-class pride but it is also a way of setting limits on what is and what is not 'right' for their social group. Tracy's parents are saying that her career choice does not 'fit' with their class habitus; her occupational position will not fit with their shared class disposition. Tracy's parents are therefore perpetuating class distinctions and norms; they are adhering to the state of play, thereby committing a type of symbolic violence (Huppatz, 2010).

## Gender capital

Although the middle-class and working-class nurses identified different motivations for entering nursing, many of the nurses discussed what I consider to be 'gender capital' in relation to access to, and success within, the occupation. Similar themes arose in all their narratives including, 'feminine and female bodies', 'a necessary sisterhood', 'emotional competence and caring dispositions', and 'masculine capital, male capital and the parameters of feminine and female privilege'. The following part of this chapter is organised according to these themes.

## Feminine and female bodies

Many of the female nurses discussed the significance of their gendered bodies in one way or another. For example, the women who are studying nursing anticipate that 'being female' will help them gain and maintain employment in the occupation and many of the enrolled nursing students see the feminisation of the job as an indication that employers are more likely to hire women. For example, Janet predicted that she will have an advantage because ... *I think a lot of patients like to have women nurses* ... In addition, many of the women who had already been working in the occupation for some time also suggested that their gender had assisted in obtaining employment. In particular, this seems to be the opinion of the older female nurses because nursing was a completely unacceptable occupation for men when they began training. As Mary stated, nursing was *strictly a female dominated profession*.

I would like to suggest that this advantage occurs because caring continues to be aligned with the female body and with femininity. Therefore, caring is considered a natural and innate feminine pastime, just as it was in the Nightingale era. These associations enable women's employment and exclude men; women are *trusted* to perform in the role whereas men are regarded with *suspicion*. Caring is considered to be un-masculine and disassociated with male bodies; it tends to be divorced from hegemonic masculinity but is part-and-parcel of hegemonic femininity. Hence, to a certain extent, feminine capital is legitimated within this occupation. Within this occupation it is converted into economic capital – it may achieve economic rewards and job security.

In contrast, most of the male nurses discussed how their bodies were sometimes a disadvantage in gaining *entry* into the field. This is especially the case for areas of nursing where the majority of the patients are female:

> *I thought about midwifery, but I think there would be a disadvantage there. I mean it's all about tits and fannies. Women will be uncomfortable to have a man, whereas even a woman who hasn't had children would be more acceptable, they wouldn't like a man telling them how to give birth. ... Compared to a male obstetrician ... we are not there yet*
>
> (Russell)

Russell therefore suggested that because midwifery deals with female anatomy, nurses who have female anatomy are assumed to be better equipped to work in this area and more acceptable to patients.

## A necessary sisterhood

Many of the female nurses also stated that their gender had worked (or will work) to their advantage within the field specifically in the care of female patients and when management is female. For example, Janet stated that her gender might assist her in achieving employment in a women's hospital:

> ... I think a lot of patients like to have women nurses, especially women. Like if you were going to the women's hospital it is more than likely that that would play a bigger role.

Abigail echoed Russell in that she stated that women are particularly favoured in the area of midwifery. However, Abigail stated that this is because female patients are now rejecting 'medical model' births that are overseen by male doctors:

> ... many women feel more comfortable with a woman and that's backed with lots of women wanting midwifery care and that means female care not doctor care, and doctors are generally male in our area.

Abigail therefore made a more sophisticated argument than Russell – rather than simply implying that this is a feminised specialisation because midwifery is concerned with female anatomy, she argued that female-dominated midwife care is preferred by women as part of a larger struggle to alter the gender order – it is part of a resistance to men controlling female bodies. Hence, the female nurses tended to suggest that women prefer to be cared for by other women and that this is recognised by employers and that women generally prefer to employ women. In nursing then, gender capital appears to provide social connections that enable employment.

In addition, half of the nurse managers stated that their gender assisted in gaining management positions. For example, Louise stated:

> I think from the point of view of within the profession ... it's still very much female dominated even though there are more and more males now. So I think as I moved into those more senior positions it was probably more acceptable because I was female ...

On a slightly different bent, Alice stated that 'being female' helped her achieve her management position because her female employees could relate to her – they recognised her disposition as akin to their own:

> *I think that's because they* (Alice's female employees) *are more comfortable working with a female because they think well ... she may have been there, done that before ... so she's more understanding because it's coming from a female perspective rather than a male you know. ... You're having hassles with your children or bringing them up and running late. Well, you know a man doesn't necessarily ... he just leaves home.*

Alice was also appointed to a management position because the male manager did not work out:

> *... there was a male in my position before I got this position and the nurses didn't relate like they relate to me. So I presume there was a 'you be the female' gender issue here.*

Therefore, it seems that female clients, female employees and female employers, in some way, privilege the female and it appears that this provides work for women and for some women assists in promotion. The more senior women in the nursing hierarchy demonstrated how this capital can be used to change their positions, climb the field's hierarchy, and perhaps gain some mobility. 'Femaleness' (or more specifically, being hailed as female) enables social connections and so is converted to social capital which then provides economic capital.

Female, but not necessarily feminine capital is at work here, female (but not necessarily feminine) bodies are privileged. Moreover, these narratives demonstrate that female employers in particular, are playing a part in reproducing the caring field as female and producing female capital. These women are actively making the female matter – they are creating the conditions under which 'femaleness' can act as capital. Women are producing a social network '... in order to produce and reproduce lasting and meaningful relationships that can secure material or symbolic profits (see Bourdieu 1982)' (Bourdieu, 1986: 52) that are derived from female capital. They are therefore participating in a struggle in order to determine the rules of play within the occupation (Huppatz, 2009).

However it is important to consider the context in which this 'privileging' of the female takes place, and whether or not this process is equivalent to the privileging of maleness and masculinity that occurs in a range of areas of social life. It may well be the case that female clients or patients, female employees and female employers would not need to privilege women if an equitable power relationship existed between the genders; there would be no need to 'protect' female employment and female clients or patients and employees would not feel more comfortable with women. Moreover, men now hold the top jobs within nursing. This means that there are a limited number of powerful women who may protect female capital. It also means there are limits to a capital which is derived from 'femaleness' or femininity (Huppatz, 2009).

### Emotional competence and caring dispositions

The majority of the female nurses asserted that in order to be competent at their job, a nurse must display various skills and competencies and they tended to associate these skills and competencies with femininity. These skills and competencies are mostly stereotypes of femininity. Nonetheless, according to most of these women, these skills and capacities enable them to know the game of the occupational space and play it well, albeit within limits. Hence, the feminising of these skills and competencies provides these women with confidence in their capacities and, as a result, their femininity becomes an asset.

For the most part, the feminine skills and capacities that the female nurses referred to were emotional competencies and caring dispositions which are seen by the female nurses as either learned through socialisation or as a biological artefact. For example, the women often linked them capacities to their mothering roles. Cynthia stated:

> *Maybe, because I'm a mother as well and some of the skills you use in mothering you also use in nursing.*

Similarly, Janet commented:

> *... nurturing, caring ... being in childcare I sort of understand what people's needs are. And because I've had children of my own.*

The nurses therefore likened nursing to mothering, just as its founders did. In addition, as they naturalised caring as feminine the female nurses sometimes also devalued men's emotional competencies. For example, Julie stated: *... men have the ability to be caring but it's not as instinctive.*

Therefore, whether they are conceptualised as natural or not, emotional competencies, particularly a caring disposition, appear to be feminine capitals that operates in this occupation. Illouz (1997) and Reay (2004) argue that emotional capital is gendered, in that women carry more of this resource than men. As I stated previously, I would also like to argue that emotional capital is a feminine capital. Emotional competence is viewed as a feminine disposition because it is associated with mothering and aligned with the female body. Doing emotion work well is doing femininity well. As the nurses themselves have pointed out, females are socialised to do emotion work, they are encouraged to do this work both in the private realm and in the public ream, they are rewarded for emotional competence, and by the time they are adults many women are very experienced and accomplished at this work. Males, in contrast, do not tend to be encouraged to invest in emotional competencies as associations with femininity makes them 'un-masculine'.

Other nurses talked about feminine competencies in relation to management roles rather than caring for patients. Abigail stated that the feminine quality of intuition makes women better negotiators in her field:

*I see them as feminine, women are quite canny (laughs), they can … they have lots of intuition and I guess that women's intuition, women's ways of knowing and all those sorts of things are very important with how or when you broach topics for implementing change for example, things like that.*

Here, her mention of 'intuition' suggests that she is capable of sensitivity to the emotions of others and to withhold her own emotions and opinions so as to carry out negotiations that benefits her within social interactions. Again, Abigail is talking about emotion work.

Other nurse managers discussed gendered competencies that are not quite emotion work in that they do not entail the management of the emotions of others but they do entail the self-disciplined management of their own emotions. For example Christine discussed her capability for stamina and resilience:

*… mental stamina, I think that tends to be a sort of female trait and definitely again, that's a good fit with nursing, sticking to things and making sure they get done and just keep coming back even if some days aren't good – a mental resilience I guess to deal with things even though they're not always pleasant.*

This is interesting because women are often seen as 'soft' while men are seen as 'hard' and therefore more competent at resilience. As Alvesson (1991: 976) argues 'Low resilience appears to be a standard discourse about women in relation to many kinds of work (Cf. Marshall and Wethereall, 1989)'. In this way Christine argues against common understandings of femininity.

Hence, the female nurses did share many positive stories of feminine advantage. However, the women's conceptualisations of their skills as traits and instinct also work against them. Although their recognition of their feminine capacities and competencies appears to give women the confidence to play 'the game' of the occupation, their naturalisation of these capacities reinstates the doxic order in which the feminine is subordinated to the masculine.

In addition, the result of this naturalisation of feminine capital is that feminised occupations continue to be undervalued and underpaid because these feminine skills are not seen as acquired skills and capacities but as an innate female capacity. Indeed, this is why nursing lobby groups and activists, in an attempt to raise the status of their jobs, have attempted to highlight the scientific and technical aspects of their work.

Furthermore, because of the dichotomous nature of the gender order women's confidence in these 'natural' capacities might simultaneously equate with a diminished confidence in less stereotypical capacities and thereby limit their practice. For many women, femininity is not a tool that may be taken up whenever needed, it is often incorporated into women's selfhood so that they are 'feminine selves' who stand in opposition to 'masculine selves'. In sum, femininity, when thought of in this way, is a sort of 'double-edged sword', it may operate as a capital but these perceptions reinstate gender norms and hierarchies and limit women's actions (Huppatz, 2009).

Furthermore, despite the female nurses' depictions, these assets are not exclusive to women. Although emotional competencies are feminised, the male nurses do appear to draw profitably on both masculine and feminine dispositions and performances; many of the male nurses discussed how they also wield what I perceive to be feminine capital. In particular, they too discussed how their caring dispositions enable them to do their jobs well. For example, when asked 'are the characteristics which make/will make you good at your job related to gender?' Stan replied:

*Ah … that's an interesting question. If I had to compare my maleness to people outside of the health field … then I'd say I have more feminine characteristics ... not in my behaviour but in how I look at things. I have a more nurturing role. Or a more nurturing approach to things than to say my partner's son-in-law who works for* (name of brewery). *If I look at those sorts of people in my family ... my brother-in-law or my nephew, my nurturing skills and appreciation for human need would come from a mothering perspective. Which is not the nurturing skills that those people have, you know what I mean?*

Here, as with many of the female nurses, Stan discussed how he embodies a feminine emotional disposition which advantages him in nursing. In addition, Stan, like the female nurses, connected mothering with emotional competence and femininity yet he moves outside of the norm in that he disconnected mothering from female bodies and aligned it with his own. Furthermore, he compared his disposition with the dispositions of men in other jobs suggesting that his disposition is either a characteristic of men who work in health care or is produced by the health care industry as an 'occupational effect'; Stan's comments indicate that his occupation is significant in shaping his gender.

Similarly, Russell stated:

*Yes, because I'm not a really masculine guy, I'm not a really blokey bloke and I always get along with women, I'm a soft gentle kind of guy. If I'd been a construction hard man there would be no way I could go into nursing ... I don't think it's a career for a really macho guy, because you've got to do ... I don't think they would cope, although plumbers clean up poo. Maybe it's the caring aspect, they aren't able to show caring and compassion and that is part of the job ...*

Russell gets along with women, he is *gentle* and *caring* and *compassionate*. He is also emotionally competent. However, he disassociated these competencies with masculinity, despite his embodiment of these characteristics. Russell also reinstated the division of labour in his narrative and aligned construction with 'machoness' and 'hardness' thereby distancing it from femininity. Nevertheless, Russell indicated that macho men *aren't able to show caring and compassion* – they avoid care work because of social sanctions rather than a lack of biological imperative.

This is evidence that men engage in both feminine and masculine practices – they do not necessarily have monolithic gender identities. This may also be evidence of change in the way that masculinity is constituted, perhaps what is happening here is the "emergence of a more fluid, bricolage masculinity" (Gill 2003 39)' (33). What is more, this may be evidence that 'increasing numbers of men may be appropriating femininity and feminine ways of being in order to increase their mobility in the labour market (Adkins, 2002)' (Reay, 2004: 65). As I shall show later in this chapter, the male nurses discussed profiting from both masculine *and* feminine capital. So while the female nurses mostly limit themselves to feminine practices and identities, the male nurses are employing multiple gender identities and engaging in diverse gender practices.

In addition, there are some specialised areas within nursing where masculine dispositions are valued. For example, the male nurses discussed how they are advantaged in Intensive Care Units and Psychological Wards where rationality and physical strength are valued. When I asked if it was an advantage to be male in nursing Ned replied:

> *Sometimes. Typically males are supposed to be more analytic and have science based brains. And particularly when you are looking after patients in ICU ... the critically injured patients ... that comes into play ... I'm also a large man, 6 foot and well built, so I do get asked to do the lifting ...*

So it seems that the occupation is segregated within so that there are some areas where masculinity is valued. In the next section I will discuss how masculinity is particularly profitable in management.

## Masculine capital, male capital and the parameters of feminine and female privilege

As I discussed in Chapter 3, although nursing is a feminised occupations, the senior posts in the UK and Australia are disproportionately occupied by men (Glover & Radcliffe, 1998; Lewis, 2004). It seems that when men pursue management within the field they experience greater success. Although femaleness and femininity enable entrance into the field, provide female nurses with confidence in their abilities and (if women are in power) assist in promotion, within this occupation (as perhaps with most others), feminine and female capitals do not tend to dominate masculine and male capitals. This situation is understood by women and is particularly illustrated in the narratives of the female nurse managers. For example, Mavis experienced a problem of a gendered nature when pursuing management. She claimed that her gender does not operate as capital but was very reluctant to discuss the details of the blockages she encountered:

> *Q: Was it a fairly straightforward pathway for you to pursue management?*
>
> *Mavis: No not at all.*

*Q: Why?*

*Mavis: I had a particularly difficult manager who didn't just target me, he targeted a lot of people. Who, I would say, really put my career back about ten years.*

*Q: Has your gender worked to your advantage within this profession?*

*Mavis: I don't think so.*

*Q: It didn't assist you gaining a more senior position?*

*Mavis: No, in fact ... no just leave it at that.*

Similarly, when asked if her gender had worked to her advantage in achieving senior positions, Abigail stated:

> *I think it's actually tougher than what it would be if I was a man. I've seen throughout my career, fellows jump ahead in leaps and bounds, often with very minimal experience. They seem to be able to be promoted a lot faster than what women are, that's for sure.*

Some of the students were aware of these limits to the feminine and female even before they started working within the field. For example, Janet stated:

> *And I don't know about management, but I think a lot of patients like to have women nurses ...*

The female nurses' stories contrast quite significantly with the male nurses' stories of career progression. While the male nurses do not appear to see their gender as an asset in gaining entry to the field, they do seem to see male bodies and masculine dispositions as advantageous in the more prestigious specialty areas of nursing work and also in gaining promotion and management positions. For example, Ned commented:

> *Yes. I think you get noticed more as a male nurse. I don't have any overt examples when it helped though. But myself, and the male nurses I know, don't tend to be shy in coming forward. And I'm not sure but that's why you see more men in higher clinical or management positions because you (men) get on and do things ...*

> *... Male nurses are working in higher management or clinical specialities and that would be seen as a high status. ... ICU is seen as more prestigious than aged care because it's on TV ... and certainly there are more men in ICU than aged care.*

Ned suggested here that men are noticed more and are therefore promoted more frequently to high status positions; male bodies (masculine of otherwise) are set apart from female bodies and this puts men at an advantage. This is male capital at work.

Ned also indicated that men are pushier in their pursuit of high status positions. Similarly, when asked if his gender assisted him in gaining employment within this area, Stan replied:

> *Yes. ... in being promoted and that pisses me off. I am sure that men are promoted because they're men and women are just left behind. I don't really like working for men, I've had all female bosses and I prefer female bosses. Lots of men get up there and I detest the fact ... I mean the Nurses Association – there's a male in charge ... I mean 'hello'. I think that gender promotes those people. And most women these days cope quite well with kids and being in charge. So I don't like the idea that women don't get to the top of the tree.*
>
> *... I think men are more pushy and aggressive and they promote themselves more. I mean that's what I hate about working with men because I come up with a good idea and suddenly it's theirs. So they get credit for what you came up with. So men push themselves and they tread on women. And they lie, and manipulate and are deceitful.*

Stan proposed that men are ambitious and competitive and this puts them at an advantage in pursuing senior positions. Therefore masculine qualities enable the achievement of senior positions within this occupation; they operate as capital. For these reasons the male nurses are unlike the female nurses in that their progress to management and speciality positions was straightforward. For example, Stan (a nurse manager) stated:

> *Yes, it (promotion) was a natural process that occurred in every job I had.*

The male nurses also talked about how they use feminine competencies to their advantage in management. Stan suggested that he was promoted because he was recognised as male but he is a good manager because of his feminine disposition. When asked if the characteristics that made him good at his management role are masculine or feminine he stated:

> *I think they're more feminine. It's really interesting, and I hate that I even have this thought but I always think of the masculine things as the tough parts as in 'I have to sack you or discipline you' ... and all the other stuff, the good management stuff is the feminine stuff ... but that's the way it is ... I've been socialised.*

Therefore Russell and Stan's willingness to take on different gender dispositions appears to get these men ahead. What is more, as Adkins (2005) suggests, their embodied labour may be more readily recognised as labour because it is not as likely to be naturalised. Their success suggests that while both men and women may wield feminine capital, men may have more control over how their performances are received by audiences (patients and employees). This capital is therefore more useful to men than it is to women. However, it must be recalled that their parents and friends disapproved of their decisions to pursue nursing, their participation in this occupation seems to damage their social relationships outside of the occupation and this is because they are not seen to be 'doing gender well'. By doing femininity these men are not seen to be doing masculinity well and this reduces their masculine capital and jeopardises their social standing.

## Conclusions

In this chapter I have examined how women's decisions to enter nursing often appear to be directed by the feminine habitus and doxic system; 'doing nursing' is often 'doing femininity'. In particular, it seems that nursing 'fits' with those who have feminine dispositions and are middle-class. However, there are exceptions and in particular, working-class women and men seem to pursue nursing for economic stability and mobility.

This chapter has also demonstrated that female capital and feminine capital are experienced profitably in this occupation; female bodies, feminine bodies and emotional competence and caring dispositions all operate as capital. Women are aware of this and this knowledge plays a role in their career choices. However, feminine and female capitals do not dominate masculine and male capitals, and men continue to hold the top jobs in nursing. While middle-class women might have a better 'feel for the game', this does not mean that they travelled easy roads into management. Their gender made it *tougher*, and even set Mavis' career back ten years. This means that they do not unproblematically own and exchange gender in the workplace (Adkins, 2005). Further, feminine capital is seen as incompatible with masculine capital and diminishes men's masculine capital and social standing outside of the occupation. Femininity is a capital but within nursing it operates within limits.

The next chapter, Chapter 6, moves on from nursing and looks at worker's experiences pursuing and working within social work. Chapter 6 look at the specificities of gender, class, and gender capital experiences in social work but it also looks at the commonalities between nursing and social work, suggesting that these two occupations may be part and parcel of the same 'field' of social action.

# 6
# Social Work

As I discussed in Chapter 3, social work and nursing share similar cultures, demographics and histories. Social work, like nursing, is a feminised respectable middle-class 'caring career' and a connection is often made between social work, caring and femininity. These correlations resulted in similar themes occurring throughout the nurses' and social workers' narratives in regard to motivations, pathways and gender capital experiences, and this chapter is therefore organised along similar lines to the nursing chapter. Indeed, this chapter will demonstrate and conclude that both occupations occupy the same field: the field of 'paid caring work'. However, there is an absence of male voices and an addition of academic voices in this chapter.

## Gender stories

### The importance of caring and fit between disposition and position

As with the nurses the majority of social workers were highly motivated by a desire to care. In fact, possibly because there were no men in this cohort, this tendency was even greater for the social workers. So it seems once again, that their gendered habituses may have directed these workers' choices.

Moreover, as with the nurses, the female social workers largely experience a good 'fit' with their occupation. Female workers in this occupation appear to experience a congruency between their occupational position and gender dispositions. For example, Lisa discussed her experience of this 'fit' and also naturalised this compatibility – relating it to mothering and instinct. She also juxtaposed her experience of this work with her male partner's view of this work, creating distance between his gendered experiences and world view and her own:

*Yes, as I was saying probably the maternal mothering sort of instincts make this job a good fit for women. … there are a lot of women in the field so I think that's reflected over and over. Also, for example, my partner's cynicism about this type of work shows the gender difference in understanding of different issues, I think.*

Interestingly, for the academics, this 'fit' seems to extend to social work academia, even though academia is associated with culture and rationality (which are traditionally associated with masculinity and men). Ruth (a social work academic) stated:

*Social workers as academics I think are a different breed than sociologists, we still bring our social work persona into academia and it's a very female focussed relational thing, I suspect the social work schools are very different disciplines within the university. I haven't worked in other disciplines, it may just be a stereotype for you, but I think that's probably the case.*

Ruth therefore aligns social work academia with femaleness and sets social work academia apart from other disciplines (although sociology is a humanities and social science discipline which now also tends to be more feminised than other academic disciplines, albeit perhaps not to the extent of social work). She also aligns her occupation with femininity by stating that it is *relational*, locating her work with human interaction and emotion rather than rationality. Nonetheless, her compatibility with the occupation, gendered or otherwise has clearly enabled Ruth success, she is one of the small portion of women who have 'made it' to the upper echelons.

### Maternal worlds

About one quarter of the social workers have mothers who are or were in social work, welfare work or allied fields. Almost half the women also reported their mothers to be homemakers (carrying out unpaid caring work in the home). Holly cited a possible relationship between her practices and the practices of her mother and while she does not share her occupation with her mother, she does highlight the significance of 'maternal worlds' for creating continuity between her disposition and actions and the disposition and actions of her mother. Holly stated that she chose this career because:

> *I suppose just the more nurturing role that women take on, which I probably inherited from my mum cause she's very maternal and protective of people and I suppose that's a feminine trait in a lot of cases.*

Furthermore, it is not only the social workers' mothers who engage or engaged in gendered work. Only one of their fathers is in a feminised profession (a teacher), the majority are or were in mansculinised occupations such as building, electrical work and engineering and over half of the social workers who have partners, have male partners in masculinised occupations. So it seems, again, these women live in worlds that are highly divided in terms of paid labour, and this may have impacted their occupational choices.

### Limited choice and ordinary gender relations

Many of the social workers also discussed the role that socialisation might have played in directing their career path. Syliva talked about the significance of social expectations and role play:

> *I think back to just growing up with my cousins and my brother and my sister it was just expected that girls would do the caring things side of things and I can even remember playing doctors and nurses with my cousins, and from the word go I think we're socialised into it.*

Susan discussed the caring role that she was expected to assume as a child in her family, the confirmation of her choice as gender-appropriate by the wider community, and the sanctions that men experience for participating in this feminised job:

> *I'm sure they do in a lot of ways, I think, when I was growing up I was the only child until I was twelve and then in a period of eight years my dad and step mum had three kids and so I had a big role in … I was sort of the other carer as such. In some ways I think that probably wouldn't have happened if I was male, and so there's probably some sense in which I've been taught to play that role. … I guess it's harder to say if wider stuff has played a part in that as well, I'm sure it has in some way. It's probably also easier to be a woman in social work, it's very … there's probably under ten guys in our course out of a hundred people. People don't say 'why are you doing social work?'*

Some of the social workers were quite reflexive about their career choice falling in line with the gender order. Ruth stated *'No-one thought any differently, you just did that* (chose gendered work) ...' and Elizabeth commented: *I think that if I was a guy I probably wouldn't have chosen social work although I might've chose psychology.* Both of these women acknowledged their participation in the doxic system, which appears to have directed their career choice. However, as with the nurses who exercise this kind of clarity in regard to their choices, these women remain in the profession and continue to affirm its 'fit'.

Claudia is unique in that she is the only worker who discussed how her husband actively directed her choice. Claudia stated that her husband only accepted her career in social work because he sees it as connected to her mothering role:

> *Ah ... to be totally honest I think that he sees my job and my studies as an add-on to my roles as a mother and a wife. So ... it's sort of like giving me permission to do it rather than ... being um ... something that I naturally want to do. 'Oh well, you do that as long as the cooking the cleaning and everything else is all done'.*

> *Q: So if you made a less gendered occupational choice he would be less accommodating? Or ... ?*

> *Claudia: Yeah, I think he would be. He sees that I'm doing it for the good. I'm doing it to try and make it better for others ... other mothers (he says) with kids with disabilities and other families and mothers. It's only because he's still at home, you know ... he's ... in the shed and you know, works on gear boxes and stuff like that now and again. Of course, I do quite long hours at work and also am coming here at the library and stuff after work and I come home quite late and he's sort of started to cook tea but waited for me to come home and finish doing things ... It's funny how it sort of falls into those sorts of roles. He can get someone to help him mow the lawns, but to get someone to help to clean the house ... that's a different thing. You should be able to do that ... (laughs). It's a common story.*

Claudia's narrative indicates that she is only permitted to participate in this occupation because social work is feminised work and her husband sees it as connected to her mothering role. Furthermore, it is expected that this work does not limit her capacity to carry out her unpaid work in the home. Interestingly, as outlined in Chapter 3, the logic that Claudia's husband applies to her work role is the logic that the professions pioneers appropriated to justify women participating in the public realm. However, this is now a logic that many social workers wish to steer from away from so that it is considered a professional and worthwhile practice.

Social work is therefore a career path that is acceptable for women; it is an activity that women are encouraged to take up. And as social work is a normative career choice for women, others play a role in their decisions to pursue this work, whether through affirmation or sanction. It seems then, that once again, the 'gender order' determines what work is and what work is not appropriate for women and men and this is reinforced in everyday relations.

### Divergent dispositions: performing caring

Despite caring being a normative activity for women, some of the social workers, like the nurses, do not find emotional caring labour easy. For example, Bronwyn stated:

> *the caring side of it, I think, can be one of the most difficult things. I really don't find that easy at all. I've got pretty low bloody patience and like everyone you need your space and it's not that caring ... people can be extraordinarily difficult I don't think the caring part comes particular easy. But again I think that's sort of, if you can learn certain other skills that just falls into place as well.*

Once again, this evidence runs counter to claims that the caring role is an inherent female role and that women always embody a caring disposition. It also indicates that women do not always own feminine capital; sometimes it must be cultivated. Moreover, Bronwyn's comment gives reference to the way that performances come to be recognised as stable embodiments. As with other performances caring *just falls into place* if repeated enough times, appearing as natural. This produces a stable sense of a caring self. This is an example of how gender is produced via what Butler terms 'performativity'.

### Class stories

As with the nurses, the majority of the social workers occupy middle-class positions and are from middle-class backgrounds. As discussed in Chapter 3, it has been argued that historically, social work was a project of middle-class intervention into the morality of the working class (Mendes, 2005: 124) and was a 'calling' for women from the middle class. Further, as is the case in nursing, the prevalence of caring as a motivator for women to pursue social work may be, in part, connected to the prevalence of middle-class women in this occupation.

However, the community work students were exceptional in this group in that they identified as working class in position and background. The community students therefore share class identities with the enrolled nursing students who also study at further education colleges. In addition, and, perhaps more surprisingly, the social work academics also identified as coming from working-class backgrounds. The social work academics are therefore exceptional in that they have achieved senior positions despite their working-class histories.

Also of interest, there is a division between the students in this group, between those who are studying community welfare work via further education institutions and those who are studying social work via universities. In contrast to the further education students, the majority of the social work university students identified themselves as coming from middle-class backgrounds and occupying middle-class positions. Only one of these women saw herself as coming from a working-class background and one other saw herself as coming from a lower-middle class background. This fits with the way in which the education system is stratified; in 2003 the Australian Council of Social Services reported that only about 15 per cent of university students come from low income families (ACOSS, 2003: 2) so that university positions in Australia are primarily taken up by middle-class individuals and in the UK children from wealthiest two per cent of households are twice as likely to go to university than children from poorer households (Shepherd, 2009).

### Classed motivations

Despite the significance of caring for the social worker's career choices, many of the women discussed their career choices in economic terms. However, as was the case for nursing, economic concerns were primarily voiced by the working class, and in particular, many of the further education students stated that their career and study choices were motivated by the desire to earn more money. For example, Rosa discussed her motivations in terms of consumption: *So that's why I would like to get a job, so at least I can go in and have more purchasing power.*

Rosa anticipates that her community welfare qualification will provide her with the freedom to consume. At first glance this quote may seem somewhat obscure, but Bauman argues:

... as in all other kinds of society, the poor of a consumer society are people with no access to a normal life, let alone to a happy one.

In a consumer society however, having no access to a happy or merely a normal life means to be consumers *manquees*, or flawed consumers. And so the poor of a consumer society are socially defined, and self-defined, first and foremost as blemished, defective, faulty and deficient – in other words, inadequate – consumers.

(2005: 38)

According to Bauman (2005) then, in contemporary western society, consumption is central to 'normal' everyday life and to be a non-consumer is to be excluded from society. Therefore, Rosa is like many of the nurses in that she is attempting to put a floor in her circumstances, and if not gain high status, at least 'normal' status. Rosa simply wants to participate in consumer society.

Some of the women in more senior posts also discussed economic motivations, particularly those who have come from working-class backgrounds. Sylvia stated:

*Another, being realistic, motivation is just being able to have work that conforms with the lifestyle that. ... I'd like to think I've got a fairly simple lifestyle, but you know you need to have the financial resources to be able to do that so I suppose that's a factor too.*

Here Sylvia talked about the importance of money to preserve a middle-class position. Sylvia also suggested that she needs to maintain work that 'conforms' to her current middle-class lifestyle which is also an issue of social *status*. Once again, this occupation (especially an academic position) is middle class. Sylvia's occupation therefore helps to maintain her socio-economic and status position in society.

In addition, as with the female nurses who separated from their partners, Claudia's motivations appear to be born out of economic necessity. Claudia has deliberately sought out higher wages because she has become the primary earner in her household:

*... It may not bring in the big dollars like as if I was in accountancy or in the corporate world but in terms of social, yeah. I have tried to every time I've moved into a different position to better myself in that particular position ...*

Economic interests also sometimes featured in the social worker's discussions of promotion and promotion featured most prominently in the narratives of the university students. This is another way the university students differ from the further education students – while the university students did not tend to discuss economic interests in relation to their motivations for pursuing a social work job, they did discuss economic interests in terms of their desires to climb the social work hierarchy. A number of the university respondents stated that they aspire to work in policy rather than 'hands on' social work – because this will provide them with greater economic rewards. Justine was positive about this prospective pathway:

> ... in the long term I'm really interested in policy ... and the money is in policy, it's definitely in policy. But I've always been interested in that level of decision making in a way, so ... I'm pretty positive about that, especially in terms of living in the city, you know ... Yeah, because I'm an incredibly materialistic person and I love objects and I love clothes and love that stuff to nourish my sense of self and I love travel and I love, I love aesthetic things as well.

Justine was therefore very open about her economic interests in relation to the pursuit of a more senior position; she looks forward to the power and material rewards it will bring and the city lifestyle it will enable. Another participant, Elizabeth, described a policy role as an inevitable career progression. She sees policy work as having greater continuity with the positions of others in her family: *Well I don't hope to earn as much as my dad does in this profession, however if I changed career paths slightly I could eventually earn what he does...*

For Elizabeth, a policy position is necessary in order to approximate the economic position of her father and thereby maintain her family's economic status (and perhaps their associated social status). Here Elizabeth's aspirations appear to be reproductive of her family's class position – she expects her career pathway to be congruent with her fathers. This example also shows how, particularly now that women have entered the paid workforce, women may be impacted by 'paternal worlds' as well as maternal ones, especially when it comes to maintaining a family's class position.

The tendency for the university students to discuss economic interests in terms of promotion rather than career choice is perhaps due to the fact that these participants self-identified as occupying middle-class positions and as coming from middle-class backgrounds. Entering the field does not necessarily improve their economic positions as they are carriers of their families' class status (of which economic status is a part). However, the achievement of a *senior position* may improve their economic positions and (as occupation is an indicator of class) senior positions may also have the appropriate occupational status. Hence for these participants promotion is desired and even expected. In contrast, discussions of promotion and policy work did not feature in the narratives of the further education students; it appears that the further education students do not dare to aspire to seniority.

These differences between the participants also indicate that the middle-class habitus has a better *feel for the game* of this middle-class vocation. For example, like most of the university students, Justine identifies as coming from an upper-middle class background and Elizabeth identifies as coming from a middle-class background and their fathers occupy well-paid and senior positions. It is their families' expectations that they also achieve seniority and economic wealth in their careers but, as middle-class individuals, they also have the cultural knowhow to strive for seniority and the cultural competence to fit in with the middle-class culture which, as was discussed in Chapter 3, has characterised and appears to continue to characterise, the profession. Moreover, these differences in workers' aspirations may indicate that gender norms are less rigid in the higher classes. Perhaps, as Bourdieu (1984: 382) suggests 'socially constituted differences between the sexes tends to weaken as one moves up the social hierarchy' so that women 'women share the most typically male prerogatives'. However, these norms cannot be that much weaker because, bar these few examples, just as was the case for nursing, economic motivations did not tend to rank highly in the self-identified middle-class women's narratives. In addition, promotion only ranked moderately for the middle-class women. As with the nurses, when these women discussed the importance of economic capital it was mostly in relation to student wages (which, again, is not a permanent or accurate measure of advantage), or it only became important in situations of separation or divorce or if their partners could no longer provide the primary income.

### Reconciling money and care

It might also be noted that, again, it may be difficult or inappropriate for the middle-class women to emphasise a desire for money rather than a desire to care. For example, for Megan, reconciling her need for money with her desire to care is particularly problematic:

> *It's a big generalisation to make but it is more the devaluing economically of the kind of work social workers do and that is a factor in my decision about which kind of social work I will pursue. I mean I'm really in*

*a horrible dilemma of knowing that I'm going to need to support myself
and save money for retirement planning. But I'm going to have to consider
that when I make a career choice and yet my folks have taught me that
I will really miss face-to-face contact. I guess I kind of do resent the fact
that policy and that sort of thing is more highly valued in my career than
traditional caring, face-to-face work.*

Megan articulated her need to earn money as a *horrible dilemma* and her
parents reinforce this sentiment. Megan's *horrible dilemma* stems from
the fact that even though she is middle class, she is also a single woman
who must support herself and a desire to care therefore cannot be her
only motivation. This does not sit well with a feminine middle-class
habitus. In addition, her narrative highlights the subordination of
bodily interactive work to non-bodily work.

### Ordinary class relations

The doxic system of class classification shapes the realm of possibility
for each individual. For each individual it produces 'reasonable and
unreasonable' classed practices (Bourdieu, 1990: 77). While, social work
is a suitable occupational position for the middle-class women, one
which they are encouraged to inhabit, this is not necessarily the case for
the working-class women. For example, Ruth stated:

*I was the first person in my entire extended family to get a tertiary educa-
tion, so they would never have heard of a social worker before I took it on. …
my siblings and extended relations of our generation all are in trades and
things like that, and that's valued a lot more highly than our decision to go
into other professions/education … its more respectable … They don't
really understand what it means to go to a university. It's a different world
to them so they don't understand and they don't respect it as such. In terms
of the profession itself they think it's a strange choice that anybody would
make, getting involved with working with people who are struggling … the
depression. They've never discussed it but it's just the comments that they
make, 'why would you want to do something like that.*

Not only did Ruth's parents not encourage her to pursue this career
path, they do not recognise the *value* of her education or career path.
Ruth's parents do not recognise social work and university education
as *respectable*; these types of pursuits are not an aspect of their cultural
currency. This demonstrates the different cultural logic that operates in
middle-class and working-class fields; a trade provides greater social status
within the working-class field than a university educated profession

or academia might. This also further demonstrates the different class meanings attached to different forms of education – trade education takes place in further education institutes and these institutions are associated with the working class, professional occupational training takes place at universities which are associated with the middle class. In addition, Ruth's narrative indicates why more working-class women do not pursue social work. Working-class women like Ruth are in this line of work *despite* a lack of social approval; they have broken with the doxic system.

## Gender capital

### Feminine and female bodies

Nevertheless, despite its association with middle classness, social work is still a feminised occupation and as such, is a place where femaleness and femininity may be privileged. As was the case for the nursing cohort, many of the female social workers discussed feminine and female bodies as assets in one way or another. In particular, many of the further education students saw the feminisation of social work as an indication that this would be an area in which they had an advantage over men and employers were more likely to hire women. For example, Rosa stated that she does *think* and *hope* that as a woman she will be advantaged in the occupation. And Katherine suggested that this advantage might be due to the fact that

> *There's that traditional sense of women are good at these jobs which isn't necessarily true but I think a lot of people do still think that way.*

Similar responses came from the university students. For example when she was asked if she thinks her gender will work to her advantaged in the occupation Elizabeth replied:

> *I hope so. I need everything I can get at this stage.*

Some of the university students offered previous experiences within the occupation as evidence of feminine advantage within the occupation. For instance, it appeared that Bronwyn was of the opinion that gender capital has already worked as an asset for her in the industry:

> *But I reckon that after I quit my degree the first time and went and starting working I think it was easier to get the job that I got, being a woman ... I think because I was a girl it was easier to get into that than say if I had been a drop out guy.*

Bronwyn clarified this point in the next part of her answer:

*people are a lot more trusting of somebody coming in with no experience who's a girl to go and do the whole personal care thing and mind people.*

So in Bronwyn's opinion, common assumptions about women's capacity to care enabled easy employment. Again, female bodies are associated with feminine competencies, even before women have demonstrated that they have any propensity for this kind of labour. As is the case in nursing, many of the women in senior posts were particularly adamant that women are more likely to be hired for social work. For the older women this is because gender norms were even more rigid in the past and men who transgressed gender norms were regarded with *suspicion* for upsetting the gender order. Ruth stated:

*I think a lot of young men who did social work are looked on with suspicion in a sense. ... so, it gave me ... made a difference if I was competing for jobs with young men ...*

Again, social work, because of its association with emotional caring and femininity is aligned with women and distanced from men so that men who participate unsettle the gender order and possibly experience diminished masculine capital and social standing outside of the occupation. It seems then that feminine capital is legitimated in this occupation and converted into employment and economic capital and many social workers, like nurses, anticipate this feminine advantage when making their career choices.

## A necessary sisterhood

In certain areas of social work the clients are always women and these are areas where female social workers are particularly advantaged over their male counterparts. Rebecca stated that her gender worked to her advantage in gaining employment because she specialised in an area where male workers may be viewed as threatening by clients. Similarly, Sylvia stated that her gender helped in gaining employment in child protection. Sylvia commented:

*when I was working with child protection in the crisis service, that was highly valued the fact that you were a female because you were often working with women that were in violent situations ... I was a family support worker and in that role, yes, it would've been because I was doing live-in work with families, so yeah, gender was important there too.*

Female bodies are therefore preferred in child protection because they are seen as less threatening due to their similarity to the client's bodies and their distance from male bodies, and perhaps also because gentleness and non-violence is associated with femininity which is associated with female bodies.

Just as was the case for nursing, many of the social workers also reported that their 'femaleness' worked to their advantage when employers were women. Ruth stated:

*and it was very likely that if I applied for a job there would've been women on the panel who would've made the decision about who came in because it's the gender nature of social work. So in that sense it might have made a difference and it might have given me an advantage.*

Hence, within this occupation, female employers and managers once again play a part in the perpetuation of the feminisation of the occupation. This was also reported to be the case for social work academia. Both of the academics stated that their gender assisted them in academia because their female employers do not conventionally hire men. When asked if her gender has assisted in an academic pathway Ruth stated:

*Certainly in this school it does, since I've been here, the five years that I've been here they've never recruited a male or even a male casual teacher, I don't think ... It's a relational thing too and I think they (the women) relate well to each other here and have had bad experiences in the past with male academics, and there was an advantage in that sense – of women all looking after each other.*

Therefore, within certain institutions and within certain social work workplace cultures 'femaleness' is an advantage. However this example is exceptional, academia is practiced in the context of universities which are mostly male dominated throughout. In addition, social work management is practiced in the context of larger human service organisations in which the upper-echelons are male dominated. Later in this chapter I will describe women's experiences of discrimination within these management and academic cultures and therefore the parameters to female and feminine privilege.

### Emotional competence and caring dispositions

As I discussed in Chapter 3, at its inception, direct links were made between social work and women's caring role in the family and this logic was used as justification for women to involve themselves in this kind of work. Indeed as Walton (1975: 257) points out, social work was even considered a substitute nurturing outlet for women who were without a partner and children. This connection between social work, emotional caring and women continues. Indeed, many of the women who had just entered the occupation were banking on using their capacities for emotion work, in particular, their capacities for nurturing and empathy, as capital in this occupation. For example, Lisa stated that because women are *able to put themselves in other people's shoes and feel empathy and that sort of thing* she should do well in this line of work.

Once again, many of the women naturalised caring as something that women as opposed to men are competent in. This means that the conceptual connection between women's traditional role in the family and social work is one that is reiterated in common understandings of social work as women's work in the present day, even by female social workers. The seemingly positive side to this alignment between women and caring is that it benefits women when they seek employment in the occupation, however, the negative side to this is that, just as is the case in nursing, women's naturalisation of their competencies may limit their actions and their aspirations to pursue unfeminine endeavours.

Like the nurses, one way in which the social workers naturalised their labour is by linking it to their mothering roles. However, Claudia did not link mothering with nurturing like the other social workers did. Instead, she asserted that mothering has provided her with stress management skills and budgeting knowhow:

> *being more aware about how to budget having been a mother and a family and do all that sort of stuff has given me insight to help me in positions ... I think it's helped me stress-wise as well – to cope with a lot of issues that are thrown up front.*

Claudia's response is therefore interesting in that she did not only associate mothering and femininity with caring and nurturing. In fact, her inclusion of budgeting goes against doxic understandings of femininity (budgeting is a rational activity). What is more, she highlighted social work labour that is other than caring labour. This indicates that the caring elements of mothering and social work may be overemphasised or at least emphasised at the expense of downplaying other elements to these roles.

### Masculine capital, male capital and the parameters of feminine and female privilege

As was the case for nursing, there appears to be limits to feminine and female privilege in social work. The two academics (Ruth and Sylvia) noted the limits to their privilege. They both acknowledged that even though their gender is an asset in their social work department it is actually a hindrance for women in the broader university context. Sylvia made this comment about gender in academia:

> *I think with gender it can be a down-play because a lot can get heaped on you if you're willing and able. ... I couldn't imagine sometimes heads of schools asking a guy to ... ask what they would put on a woman academic, to go the extra bit at times.*

Therefore, although the academic participants did identify female advantage, they also identified the very specific parameters in which it takes place. Claudia (a manager in transit to academia) commented on the value of male and masculine capitals in human service organisations:

> *A couple of positions I went for a few fellas got in front of me ... but I thought I had knowledge, more understanding ... but I was told to go and get some more experience. And it was a young fella two years out of uni that got the position as the area manager! That's why I left the department and moved into local government but that's even more gendered (laughs). It's more of a boys' club in local government than state government – I found that out pretty quick (laughs)!*
>
> *Q: What sort of experiences did you have there?*
>
> *Claudia: I felt I was seen as ... that being a woman I was the one who organised some of the planning days and ... do all little bits and pieces but the other fella who was a Community Development Officer never ran round and did all those little frivolous tasks that women do, which certainly made the job a bit harder ...*

Claudia's narrative demonstrates the negative value attributed to her gender in the management cultures of government run human service agencies; male bodies and their associated dispositions are more highly valued and gendered assumptions concerning her disposition and capabilities did not operate to her advantage. These stories are not uncommon; women's stories of discrimination in management are familiar and well researched (for example see Powell and Graves, 2003). Claudia's story also, once again, indicates that middle-class women, despite their better feel for the game, do not necessarily find management positions easy to access. Their gender can make the job *a bit harder*. Claudia was designated trivial work and therefore limited power. These stories of the limits to female and feminine capitals also give some indication of why vertical segregation continues to exist in social work.

## Conclusions

In this chapter I have explored the ways in which gender and class direct women's choices to pursue social work and impact their experiences within the occupation. Many of the themes that were found in the nurses' narratives were also present in the social workers' narratives. For example, I have found that the posts in these occupations are organised in similar hierarchies and they seem to have similar relationships with the field of education. In addition nursing and social work contain similar classed and gendered practices and processes and operate according to the same rules and regulations and value similar capitals, particularly gender capitals. Furthermore, these capitals seem to be structured in similar ways: female bodies, feminine bodies and emotional competence and caring dispositions are valued in social work, and are consciously and unconsciously wielded by workers, just as they are in nursing. However, once again, female and feminine capitals operate in a limited manner and do not dominate masculine and male capitals. These findings therefore suggest that nursing and social work are both part of the same field of action; it seems that a 'field of paid caring work' may exist.

The next chapter moves on to explore a very different occupation, one that appears to have more in common with hairdressing than it does with social work and nursing, despite its feminisation – exotic dancing.

# 7
# Exotic Dancing

This chapter examines the operation of gender, class and gender capital in the occupation of exotic dancing. As I argued in Chapter 3, exotic dancing is situated in an interesting place in the workforce; exotic dancing is sex work, and was sometimes described by the dancers I interviewed as sex work, however, it is also service work or part of 'the desire industries' (Brooks, 2010: 6) as it operates 'on ideas of desire and attractiveness' and so has commonalities with retail and fashion work. Exotic dancing is also highly feminised; women tend to work in this industry while men consume its products. For this reason male stripping is a niche market and no male dancers were available to interview for this chapter.

This chapter is structured like the previous 'case study' chapters. However, this chapter focuses on the significance of a bodily aesthetic as well as certain emotional dispositions and performances for this occupation. This chapter is divided into 'gender stories', 'class stories', a discussion of 'gender capital', and 'the parameters of feminine and female privilege' but the ways in which gender, class, gender capital and limits to privilege are experienced by the workers in this chapter are sometimes quite different from the experiences of the workers discussed in the previous chapters.

Before I move on to look further at the dancers' 'gender stories' it is important to note that the dancers I interviewed are all thirty years of age and under, and they also all identify as white. The ethnicity and age of these women is not unusual. As this is an industry in which good looks are traded on and youthfulness is associated with beauty, young women dominate the occupation. In addition, other studies have shown that the stripping industry, in all its elements, is mostly white (Prince Glynn, 2010). This may have something to do with the ethnicisation of beauty, as Brooks (2010) comments, certain raced bodies are more valuable in exotic dancing than others, and in this way exotic dancing is not unlike many other areas of the labour market As McDowell, argues:

> The hegemonic idealized body that dominates not only advertising but also the labour market is a slim, fit, young – and usually white – body (Bordo 1993). Western culture provides few – and even fewer positive – images of ageing bodies and almost never of ageing naked bodies.
>
> (2009: 173)

## Gender stories

Many of the dancers I spoke with commented on the feminisation of their work. For example, Lea stated:

> *There is only one male club here. I don't think I'd do it if I was a guy it doesn't seem as appealing ... The image of the sort of guys who do it are the sort of guys I don't find very attractive. Everyone is just very buff and they don't look very good. It seems tacky ... there doesn't seem to be a place where a woman can go and hang out in a strip club during the week ... But men can go in the week and it seems more sophisticated ...*

Here Lea recognised that her career choice was directed by gender. In addition, her narrative acknowledges the gender order. According to Lea, if men work as dancers this is *tacky*, it is not normalised and therefore of poor taste. On the other hand, men's consumption of strip clubs has been so normalised, it can even be part of a man's regular routine. Moreover, Lea supports this gender order in that she sees the men who engage in this work as undesirable. Lea also acknowledged that classed meanings are attached to male and female sexualities – men can consume sexualised services and this is 'sophisticated' whereas women's consumption of the same services is not. In this way a respectable, sexually restrained and demure femininity is valorised within Lea's narrative.

In addition, another dancer, Eliza, commented that the few men who are in this industry are gay. Perhaps this is a stereotype, or perhaps it reflects reality (there does not appear to be any research on this issue). I suspect that once again, this assumption is made because men who participate in feminised work are transgressing gender norms and are therefore regarded with suspicion and due to the alignment between hegemonic masculinity and heterosexuality their sexuality is questioned.

It seems then that within this industry roles are clearly divided along gendered lines: men tend to watch while women dance. Many feminists would argue that this division reflects an unequal power relationship between men and women where women are objects and subject to men's gaze. However, some of the narratives I present in this chapter also suggest that women's experiences of the industry can be more complicated than this: women are not always the objectified while men objectify, particularly when gender capital is consciously wielded by women.

## Gendered motivations

Perhaps because exotic dancing is not as normative or respectable as social work and nursing and perhaps because exotic dancing may even be considered 'a deviant or at best a marginal occupation' (Deshotels & Forsyth, 1997: 125) there are few stories from this group of workers about long-term aspirations to enter the industry, and no stories of expectations from parents or others that they follow this career path. The incentives to participate in this work are largely economic. However, some of the dancers did discuss their motivations in terms of a desire to experience sexiness and glamour through the industry, and these are, I shall argue, gendered ambitions. In addition, as sex work is feminised and the *only* option for many women to earn a descent living (due to parenting responsibilities or a limited education, for example) their choices are in line with the gender order.

## Empowerment

Eliza is the only dancer who communicated a long-term ambition to enter this work and Eliza is unlike the other women in that this is something that she pursued after university education, to pay for a postgraduate education and then to supplement her income from Occupational Therapy (a comparatively poorly paid, feminised, yet respectable 'caring' occupation that is related to both nursing and social work). However, she is like the other dancers in that she used the notion of empowerment to explain the appeal of this line of work. Eliza talked about how the male attention and appreciation she receives in this work made her feel more confident at a difficult time in her life:

> ... *at the time I was having a hard time and I had lost all my confidence so it* (exotic dancing) *just gave me my confidence back.*

*Q: And why was that?*

*I just finished my honours degree and felt like shit. And my boyfriend had just dumped me the week before. And so I had to move back home, back to my parents. And you know when you finish your first degree you don't think you'll ever get a job and it was like 'my life's a mess'. And people can tell if you've confidence or not. And I remember my first day after dancing people kept heckling at me on the road and shouting and stuff at me. But before that no one had done that. And it's got nothing to do with being on stage, I just felt more confident after that.*

Eliza's narrative highlights how, for many women, attention from men, even if that attention is being heckled as you walk down the street, can provide a sense of self-worth. For many women, a sense of self-worth is achieved through receiving praise on their appearance, so that sexiness is linked to a sense of empowerment. Eliza highlighted what may be a common thought process among women: '... that self confidence can be achieved through conformity to beauty standards and that such conformity is rewarded with self deserved assertiveness and a better social position' (Soley-Beltran, 2003: 320 in Coy and Garner, 2010: 662).

The link between sexiness and power is also clear in another dancer's, Annelise's, comment: *When I first started dancing I hadn't had sex before. Dancing made you feel empowered – like you have power over them.* However, Annelise's comment is more suggestive of antagonistic gender relations – she does not just want to feel good about herself, she wants to have power over men. This suggests that she feels powerless in relation to men in other aspects of her life.

Eliza also pointed to how this desire for sexiness and even to participate in exotic dancing can begin at an early age:

*Q: But you thought it was glamorous?*

*Yeah, like even when you're a little girl you see Jessica Rabbit or whatever and the movie 'Showgirls'.*

Here Eliza refers directly to the influence of film on her view of exotic dancing and her occupational choice. The influence of the media and popular culture on girls' perceptions has been debated by feminist commentators and many argue that western culture has become increasingly sexualised (see for example, Levy, 2005, Coy and Garner, 2010). For example, Gill (2008) argues that 'sexual images of women in mainstream advertising and popular culture have undergone a perceptible shift in emphasis, increasingly depicting women as actively embracing, celebrating and enjoying sex-object status (Gill, 2008)' (cited in Coy and Garner, 2010: 658). And Jyrkinen (2005) argues that western culture has become 'McSexualised' (Coy and Garner, 2010: 658). As a result Gill (2003) states that sexual objectification is being reframed as sexual subjectification and it is increasingly seen as empowering for women to use their bodies for profit (cited in Coy and Garner, 2010). Hence, Annelise and Eliza are partaking in gendered choices that may be directed by their gendered habituses and informed by the doxic system.

## Glamour

As should be clear from the narratives above, the term 'glamour' was also often used to describe the appeal of this occupation; many of the women see exotic dancing as a job where they can acquire beauty and intrigue. Eliza stated:

> *It's funny, even when I was a kid I thought it was a really glamorous job and I knew I always wanted to be a dancer.*

In addition, Annelise commented:

> *When I turned 18 I started off waitressing in the club and I started off doing dancing then. I thought it looked like they were having fun and earn money too. It wasn't really about money – I thought I'd give it a go – for the attention and the crowd. The impression from the outside is that they all get along and are happy (the dancers and customers). I thought it was a fantasy world where they were glamorous and having lots of fun. Always looking beautiful and getting money left, right and centre.*

> *Q: So, what motivated you to pursue this line of work/study?*

> *I wanted attention and to be appreciated for being beautiful.*

Here Annelise talked about a desire for money, but more than this, she wants to be seen as beautiful and glamorous. According to Skeggs, (1997: 110) glamour is often an 'escape route' from the mundane and Annelise depicted exotic dancing as a glamorous 'fantasy world' which suggests that she hopes it would elevate her from her previous circumstances. Interestingly, while many view this industry as 'dirty', Annelise's use of the term 'glamour' indicates that her prior perception of the occupation was positive; to attach 'glamour' to the job is to attribute it with some respectability. Hence, by participating in this work, in particular in high-end 'gentleman's clubs' that are marketed as glamorous, Annelise is hoping that she will gain some respectability too.

## Maternal and paternal worlds

As with the workers in the other occupations, the exotic dancers' job choice is consistent with their mothers' work patterns in that, although the dancers are not engaging in the same line of work as their mothers, their mothers also work or have worked in feminised jobs. All of their mothers have carried out full-time mothering and unpaid household work or participate or have participated in paid caring working outside of the home. In addition, the dancers' partners, if male, participate in gendered work as well (for example cabinet making and engineering). The difference with this group of workers is that many of their fathers participate in feminised work too; most are in retail or paid caring. This may be due to their working-class backgrounds – increasingly, working-class jobs are feminised jobs which means that working-class men must participate in feminised occupations more frequently too. This means that there is consistency in the career choices made by these workers and their parents but occupational choice is classed (and therefore gendered) differently for this particular group.

## Class stories

The narratives featured in this chapter are from women who work in 'gentleman's clubs', table clubs and lap dancing clubs. One is a 'feature dancer' and the rest are 'house dancers' and they all work in high status, 'glamorous' areas within the industry (Gall, 2007: 82). However, unlike nursing and social work, their participation in high status positions within the industry does not correlate with middle-class histories – all but one of the dancers are from working-class backgrounds.

The common class background of this cohort is perhaps not surprising, other studies have found that the majority of exotic dancers are working class (for example see Price-Glynn, 2010; Bott, 2006) and the industry has a strong historical link to 'working classness'. What is surprising about the dancers I talked with is that the majority have very little doubt about their class backgrounds – they are quite sure about their 'working classness'. For example, as I discussed in Chapter 4, Eliza commented:

> *The area that I grew up in is a working class area and all my friends and family were working class and I was proud to be working class.*

Most of the exotic dancers are also alike in that they are aiming for mobility and were reflexive about this. Their work-life stories therefore differ greatly from the many nurses and social workers who found it difficult to reflect on their class backgrounds. However, in this way they are also similar to the working-class nurses and social workers and, as discussed in Chapter 3, perhaps this is because the under-privileged have more reason to reflect on class relations.

## Class mobility

Class mobility appears to be a major motivation for participating in this industry. All of the dancers I spoke with chose this job because they are aiming for mobility. Eliza commented:

> But I knew that I also wanted to better myself. And now I have a Masters degree and I live in Sydney and I have this different lifestyle.

Each of the dancers discussed different tactics for mobility. Eliza used dancing to raise economic capital and pay for an education (for educational capital) which was exchanged for a respectable middle-class career (occupational therapy) and she is now supplementing her modest occupational therapy wage with earnings from pole dancing. Eliza explained her income:

> So I earn $57 000 a year as an OT and as a dancer I only work on Saturdays and I make 500 on Saturdays. But I also work as a pole dancing teacher in the evenings during the week and I probably make about 300 a week from teaching pole.

Interestingly then, as occupational therapy is considered a 'caring career', Eliza takes part in two of the work cultures described in this book. However, unlike many of the nurses and social workers, she is unwilling to forego economic capital to participate in a caring career.

Eliza also talked about her choice to enter exotic dancing as a conscious and calculated decision, and she argued that her rationality is a masculine disposition:

> Q: Did your gender or femininity or masculinity play a role in this choice?

> Eliza: See I don't think I'm a very feminine person. I think it was my masculinity. Because I'm organised and I think logically about money.

Eliza is therefore like the male nurses in that she consciously embodies both masculinity and femininity and her openness to different gender dispositions appears to have assisted her economically. So as Mavin and Gandy (2011) argue, she is 'doing gender differently'.

Eliza also uses the job to expose her to a wealthy lifestyle that she would not otherwise have access to:

> *The money is good and you get to meet people of a higher status than you'd usually get to meet. ... and you'd never get to meet these people at any other time. Like, when would you get to meet a stockbroker, like never. But if you're a dancer then you can.*

Eliza is therefore hoping that proximity to a high-class lifestyle will eventually enable a high-class lifestyle. Further, Eliza worked hard to progress in exotic dancing: she is now both an exotic dancing teacher and a 'showgirl'. Eliza's plans to write a 'how to' book on pole dancing and is quick to mention that she is a showgirl not just a table dancer and that there is a hierarchy between the two, she therefore occupies a more respectable position in the industry; one that she asserts is based on strength and skill rather than simply hustling and aesthetics. She has therefore focussed on improving her position within the industry as well as her class position in the wider social arena.

Many of the other dancers, besides Eliza, who are also aiming for mobility, are using the income from exotic dancing to pay for an education. For example, Rebecca is using her dancing income to study to be a doctor and she claimed that her education (she has already completed an undergraduate degree) is already a sign of mobility:

> *Q: How would you describe your current class status?*
>
> *It kind of feels different to my family's* (status).
>
> *Q: In what way?*
>
> *I am a whole lot more educated than most of my immediate family. I suppose it depends on the family member. But neither of my parents finished high school.*

Rebecca, like Eliza, has used dancing tactically – this is not a long-term career path for Rebecca, it is simply a means to gain mobility and create distance between herself and her family's position.

Lea has a similar story and is clear about the role that exotic dancing plays or will play in her class trajectory. Lea stated:

> *It* (dancing) *made me able to do my course and I'm saving money as well. Because I'd like to invest it or buy a house. I know lots of girls who will*

*invest in a house or something like that if they're going to do it* (dancing) *for the rest of their life.*

Lea therefore has a plan – she is saving money to invest and has undertaken an education. For Lea an education and job satisfaction are particularly important aspects of mobility:

*Q: How would you describe your current class status? Is it different to what it was growing up?*

*Lea: I think it probably will be because I have had an education whereas my mum didn't. And I have had jobs that have been pretty good – they've been something that I've wanted to do. I have the potential for much more than mum.*

This correlation between job satisfaction and status that is made in Lea's narrative is also highlighted by Bauman (2005) who claims that satisfying work is major mark of distinction in contemporary society. Bauman (2005: 35) states that 'work as self-fulfilment' ... has become the privilege of the few; a distinctive mark of the elite ...'

Lea stated that exotic dancing is full of women, like her, who are trying to move class position. She stated that among her colleagues *One is studying Chinese medicine and is financing her business. And another girl is studying to do nursing ... I know lots of girls who are like me ...* Lea therefore sees the industry, at least the high-end clubs, as an avenue for class mobility, for women to 'get ahead'.

Kristin, like Eliza, has used exotic dancing to gain access to the paid caring field and it is this, her entrance into a respectable middle-class occupation, rather than money that has improved her position. Although nursing may pay less it is more respectable and rewarding than exotic dancing: *I think I'll finish dancing when I've finished my degree ... it feels much better coming home after a birth than it does after dancing ... .* Nursing is unlike exotic dancing in that it is mostly considered 'clean' rather than 'dirty'; good women do nursing and so Kristin will feel better about herself in a nursing position. This comment reaffirms understandings of nursing as a respectable, middle-class occupation. Moreover, Kirstin's narrative is like Lea's in that she highlighted the significance of job satisfaction for a 'good life'.

As they are all aiming for mobility, all of the exotic dancers I interviewed appear to be 'goal oriented' or 'transient dancers' and perhaps have more choice than 'career dancers' (Mestemacher and Roberti (2004) and Philaretou (2006) in Mavin and Gandy, 2011). However, it is important to note that many exotic dancers do not achieve mobility through this occupation, particularly those who work in less prestigious establishments:

> *I think a lot of girls* (dancers) *could do something better with their money. It's a pity there's not some kind of education about investment or something for them.*
>
> *(Lea)*

And it is difficult to be single-minded about accumulating other types of capital or to engage in other fields because a dancing income is so generous:

> *But it's easy to get stuck in it* (dancing) *because make so much money ... There's not as much pressure to go into real world.*
>
> *(Lea)*

Therefore, while economic capital is readily available in high-end clubs, participating in the industry is not necessarily a straightforward pathway to class mobility. In addition, exotic dancing does not always prove to be a temporary career path.

### Employment benefits

These 'class stories' make it clear that a high income and class mobility are primary motivators for pursuing work or a career as a dancer. In addition, the narratives also suggest that there are other advantages to working in this area, even though they are not as obvious as the advantages of working in a 'caring field'. For example, as workplaces, strip clubs can be an improvement on other options available to working-class women. This was made clear during a conversation with Rebecca:

> *Q: ... you've come to the conclusion that it's not exploitative?*
>
> *I don't think it is. Or at least I don't think it is necessarily. I'm aware that it can be sometimes but I think to assign that to the sex industry in particular is not quite right because any work can be exploitative sometimes. And if anything I'm in a much more powerful position now than when I was doing market research. And it kind of sucks that it's when I'm in this position too, because I'm gaining much more valuable skills in this too than any other time.*

*Q: And do you feel more empowered in this than market research because you enjoy your work or you pick your hours or ...?*

*Those things. And also one of the managers actually notices when you're doing a good job and rewards you for it. So it's more individual and so on. I don't feel more empowered as a woman in particular but it certainly, for me personally, is a better workplace.*

So for Rebecca this is a more rewarding work choice than the other options available to her and for this reason she suggests that sex work is not necessarily disempowering. Exotic dancing may not be empowering for her as a woman but it is empowering as a worker because it involves flexibility in work hours and encouragement and rewards from her superiors. In fact, it *sucks* for Rebecca that she finds the treatment so favourable because the 'unrespectability' of this work makes it an unsustainable career path if she desires class mobility.

For many women dancing is also where they can seek employment and a descent wage without any formal qualifications:

*And it's easy to make a lot of money really quickly without particular skills ... (Kristin).*

A particular feminine aesthetic is the primary prerequisite for this type of work and for this reason it is a good option for women who do not have many other resources available to them. For Annelise, this aspect of the industry became very obvious when she opted out of dancing and for this reason she is considering re-entering the field:

*I look now and there's no jobs I want to do and get $15 dollars an hour. I would not want to sit here like I'm struggling now – why would I not do it (dancing) when I can get that kind of money.*

Exotic dancing pays much better than any other type of work that is within Annelise's reach. This aspect of the job also makes it appealing to immigrants who are unskilled or waiting on visas:

*It has completely changed my economic position because you need a job when you immigrate. I don't know what I would have done otherwise ... I don't know how people survive. I was waiting for a defacto visa and no one wants to employ you. And it was a good year and a half that I had to wait. I always say it's an immigrant job (laughs). Pole dancing is like being a taxi driver (laughs).*

(Eliza)

Many of the dancers also talked about the flexibility of this type of work; they discussed how they may cancel their shifts at the last minute or opt out for a while to go travelling and yet be secure that they will still have work. This might also enable mobility, as it is particularly compatible with study:

> *Now that I'm going back to uni there's no chance of getting a normal job. So it's* (dancing's) *good like that*
>
> (*Rebecca*)

> *I like the fact that it is flexible and I can work whenever I want. And also I don't feel like I'm letting anyone down if I don't want to work one night. So that's really good when I'm studying. Also I have lots of clinical placement when I can't work.*
>
> (*Kristin*)

Having autonomy and being 'your own boss' is also an appealing aspect of the job for those who are self-employed or freelance workers as is the case in the UK and the state of Victoria in Australia:

> *I like that I'm my own boss ... how hard I work is how much money I make. I choose when come in and don't have to work long hours.*
>
> (*Lea*)

> *And I like sort of being my own boss.*
>
> (*Kristin*)

> *I like being my own boss. Rather than bossed around.*
>
> (*Lea*)

> *In Melbourne you're working for yourself which makes you even more determined to earn money.*
>
> (*Annelise*)

This autonomy is not something that would be experienced in many of the jobs that are available to the working class and it gives a sense of freedom and accomplishment.

Hence, there are a number of 'upsides' to this job besides the income. However, exotic dancing is unlike nursing and social work in that most of these advantages are due to the working conditions rather than any status that might be achieved from participation in the occupation. In addition, it must again be noted that these women work in high-end clubs and so their experience is not necessarily representative of all women's experiences in this industry and as I will discuss later in the chapter, the workers also mentioned many unfavourable aspects of the working conditions too.

### Client networks/social capital

The relationships that can be fostered through this type of work also make the job appealing. Networks can be formed with clients and interactions with clients can also provide the dancers with self-esteem:

> Q: *What about your clients? Is there any kind of reward from them?*
>
> Rebecca: *They're pretty complementary. I get kind of a big head from them (laughs). And it's possible if they particularly like you or see some potential in you then other areas of your life can benefit from their help.*

Eliza also commented on meeting men outside of her class group and lifestyle and how this sometimes generates job opportunities:

> And it's funny you meet so many people ... when I went home for Christmas I worked at (a high-end club) in London and like you're a traveller and you'd never get to meet these people at any other time. Like, when would you get to meet a stockbroker, like never. But if you're a dancer then you can. In London I got to meet all these crazy stockbrokers and famous people ...
>
> Q: *So have you made any connections that have helped your life in other ways?*
>
> Eliza: *Yeah. I've made loads of good friends and I know almost everyone in the industry and I've made a real job out of teaching pole. But I've also met ... when it was my first year in Sydney someone gave me a job as a scientist so they gave me employment. A real job. It's happened to loads of people, loads of girls. The customers always want to know more about your life and it's like, 'well, I can help'.*

So it seems that sometimes beneficial connections or social capital can be acquired through dancing, providing access to wealthy cultures and new job opportunities. Money is not the only asset that this job provides.

### Gender capital

Many of the exotic dancers discussed what I consider to be 'gender capital' in relation to access to and success within their occupation. Like the nurses and social workers, the exotic dancers spoke about feminine and female bodies and emotional competence and the following section is organised according to these themes as well as others. However, the composition of these capitals in some ways differed, and differed quite drastically, from what is advantageous in nursing in social work.

### Female and feminine bodies

It seems that both female and feminine capitals are currency within exotic dancing. Many of the dancers talked about how a female body, almost any female body, can find work in a strip club, within certain limits:

> *I think there is quite a range in girls ... in how attractive they are. But I'm aware that there is a limit. Like you can't be too fat or you're not going to make any money even though there might be people out there that find you attractive. Because you need to appeal to the most number of people possible. Which is why I wear a wig as well. There will be people who will find me attractive with short hair or no hair but most people prefer long hair so that's what it is (laughs)*
>
> (*Rebecca*)

However, the dancers also talked about how *feminine* bodies are particularly profitable. Kristin talked about the selling power of a feminine aesthetic:

> *Q: So do you think your body helped you in gaining employment?*
>
> *Yes. I guess, obviously boys like to look and talk to naked girls and the more you fit the stereotype of being feminine the more helpful it is ... Also dressing and looking feminine.*

Feminine bodies are so significant for this job that they outweigh dancing:

> *Q: So do you think your body helped you in gaining employment?*
>
> *Yes. ... There are some girls who are awful dancers ... (but) they have the right body and the right hustling skills.*
> (*Rebecca*).

Bodies are therefore the main commodity in this industry, particularly those that fit into a *stereotype* of femininity. As a consequence women in this line of work put a lot of effort into making their bodies *more* gendered, into making sure that they fit into a certain feminine ideal.

As Mavin and Gandy (2011) discuss this means that 'doing gender' well is an important aspect of exotic dancing as well as sex work more generally. For example, the dancers discussed the work that they put in to maintaining slim bodies that appear untouched by the effort of their performances. If this type of body is not maintained these workers risk dismissal:

*Q: Do you have to work out?*

*Eliza: You do. Like there has been girls who have been sacked for being overweight and but I've never been overweight so. But all of us on a whole need to make sure we don't get overweight and don't get lots of bruises from pole dancing.*

A number of dancers also talked not only about the value of long hair, but also about investing in blonde hair:

*But I suppose I dyed my hair because people love blonde hair so.*

*(Eliza)*

And big breasts:

*Like if you have blonde hair and big boobs on Saturdays then they don't really have to do too much as well. So I'm aware that there are a whole lot of girls who make a lot of money every week just doing those days.*

*(Rebecca)*

These narratives show the limited feminine aesthetic that is presented and capitalised on in the clubs in which these women work. Long blonde hair and big breasts are, of course, characteristics of hegemonic femininity; they are characteristics of an idealised, sexualised, white femininity. As stated previously, beauty is ethnicised and so it is not surprising that a white ideal is more likely to be bought and sold. Mary Trautner (2005) also argues that these depictions of femininity are classed. In her study Trautner (2005) found that if dancers work in clubs that cater for white, middle-class men (as these women do) they cultivate thin, tan bodies 'with blonde hair and breast implants' and these dancers tend to cover their bodies and 'accentuated their eyes'. In contrast, Trautner (2005: 774) has found that women who work in working-class clubs are not necessarily white, often have 'more robust figures', wear less clothing, and use 'makeup to accentuate their lips'. So it seems that the aesthetic presented depends on the customers and as a result, the women in Trautner's (2005: 774) study, just as in this one, 'came to embody the raced and classed femininities evoking "different amounts of cultural and educational capital"'.

In addition, the employment of women who embody or perform high-class femininity adds to the glamour of high-end clubs and has the affect of normalising the environment. As Shulman (2011: 24) has found: 'Many establishments market themselves as gentlemen's clubs and have expensively decorated interiors. Expensive decoration normalises the sexual service and undercuts moral reservations (for health and safety qualms) a customer may have in relation to purchasing the sexual service'. 'Expensive' interiors and bodies equate with respectability and therefore make workplaces less deviant whereas cheap interiors and bodies equate with unrespectability.

*Plastic surgery*

Having 'the right body' and evoking this raced and classed sexualised femininity, is partly about dress and make-up but mostly it is anatomy that is on display in strip clubs, and as the discussions above indicate, some women's anatomy is clearly viewed as more feminine than others within this context. As a consequence, many women must engage in plastic surgery in order to create hyper-feminine bodies that fit with this ideal. This means that plastic surgery is commonplace in this industry; dancers raise economic capital and then invest in plastic surgery (to produce feminine bodily capital) which is then traded for more economic capital:

> *I get the impression, less in this club than others, but there is lots of fake boobs. And nearly everyone tans somehow either realistically or spray tan or ... in the change rooms before they go out. But it's something I feel less comfortable doing.*
>
> *(Rebecca)*

Eliza also commented on this:

> *Q: Are there many women who get plastic surgery?*
>
> *Oh, I'm so fed up with seeing it. Yeah, loads of them. So many girls are so dumb and they get it for the job. It's gross. Lips, boobs, tattoos, I'm so fed up with the whole thing.*

It might be observed from the quotes above that not many of the dancers admitted to investing in cosmetic surgery themselves. Perhaps this is because doing so would somehow make them less feminine – their feminine bodies would not be 'natural'. In fact, Annelise was the only dancer who talked about her investments in surgical enhancement:

> *You want to know you're doing the best you can to earn the most you can. If you don't earn lots of money it's on you so you put lots of effort in (to looking good). ... I just had lip filler and filler on my eyes. But there were girls who got boob jobs.*

However, some dancers did comment that investing in surgical body alterations could be a false economy because their customers do like (limited) diversity and it is advantageous to have a point of difference. Eliza commented that surgical enhancement is most beneficial in other areas of 'sex work':

> *It might help them get magazine shoots and win competitions. And like x-ray issues – gives them the whole porn look and they'll get money that way. But as a dancer, guys either like fake boobs or real boobs. Just like the brunette or blonde thing.*

The marketability of both 'fake' and 'real' breasts as well as the disinclination among the workers that I spoke with to have surgery (or to admit that they have had surgery) may also be suggestive of the class position of the clientele in the high-class clubs in which these women work. Breasts implants are sometimes considered 'cheap' among the wealthy elite, even though they might be expensive, as they are associated with manufactured femininity and excessive sexuality and therefore distanced from middle- and upper-class femininities that are, in contrast to working-class femininities, represented as 'natural' and 'restrained'.

As a final side point for this section, it may be recalled from Chapter 2 that Bourdieu (1984) asserted that working-class women are not aware of the market value of their beauty. The narratives here disprove this argument. However, if Bourdieu is correct in that awareness of the value of beauty is *largely* a middle-class practice, then these women may be improving their social positions just by demonstrating that they too are aware of this cultural asset. As Bott (2006: 34) argues, when working-class women cultivate their bodies according to beauty norms they may gain more respectable positions in society because of the association that is made between this practice and middle-class femininity. The bodily investments made by these workers may be profitable both inside and outside this occupation.

## Emotional competence and hustling skills

Although female and, in particular, sexualised hyper-feminine bodies are the most obvious assets in this field, they are not the only gender capitals at work here. Dancers perform exaggerated sexualised femininities, and this is achieved through body work but it is also achieved through modes of interaction (Mavin and Gandy, 2011: 11). Dancers perform 'gender scripts' of men's sexual fantasies in clubs through flirtatious talk and emotion work.

Exotic dancers need to be happy, flirtatious, and entertaining but they also need to 'read' clients and exhibit 'care'.

> *It's easy to get a job you only have to go in and have a chat. A very easy industry to get into. You just have to have good social skills.*
>
> (*Annelise*)

> *I guess being friendly helps as well. Confident, friendly, happy or whatever. Being able to interact with people.*
>
> (*Kristin*)

As Rebecca mentioned, 'hustling skills' are as important as having 'the right body' in achieving a sexualised hyper-femininity. Similarly, Annelise commented: *To keep customers you have to talk ... not just be good looking.*

These skills are also more important than dancing:

> *The biggest earners couldn't dance at all. It's nice to show off but it's about the floor.*
>
> (*Annelise*)

They can even overcome age limitations that are associated with feminine bodily capital:

> *It's about personalities and how they talk. There are some girls who are really beautiful and don't make that much money. ... One of the top girls is 37 and looks ok but not great but has that aura that you listen to her ... She's confident.*
>
> (*Lea*)

So, this job is similar to other types of paid caring work in that employees are required to engage in emotion work and the more competent the workers are at this, the more money they earn. This means that caring dispositions and 'emotional competence' are capital in this occupation.

Some of the dancers discussed the significance of being caring or performing caring in a similar fashion to the nurses and social workers:

> *I guess being good at listening and talking ... caring and being caring or coming across as that.*
>
> (*Kristin*)

Here Kristin used the same terms that were adopted by those in the paid caring field to talk about her work. However she is more willing to reference performance, while those in the paid caring field tended to discuss caring as an innate skill (although, as I demonstrated, there is evidence that nurses and social workers perform caring too).

This emotion work is articulated by some of the women as being a social service, one that helps clients and gives the dancers a sense of fulfilment:

> *They're (the customers) not all freaks and they're actually people. Lots of them are lonely people that want company. A strip club is a place you sit down and have some company.*
>
> (*Annelise*)

> *I know one extreme example of a friend of mine who has a customer who comes in every week and doesn't have friends or social skills and he gets a lot of enjoyment and she is trying to encourage him to get other interests and get other friends. So I guess when people get regulars who can vent to you.*
>
> (*Lea*)

Many of the dancers who did discuss caring and emotional competencies also saw these as gendered skills or feminine skills, albeit without reference to 'mothering' or 'nurturing'. For example, Kristin suggested that 'caring' is an aspect of the femininity that is valued in the industry. However, others, like Rebecca, talked about their emotional and communicative competencies as 'hustling'. And this term is more suggestive of performance as well as manipulation:

> *the right hustling skills, like eye contact is so important, it doesn't really matter what you're doing with your body if they're looking at your face ... if you know how to talk and create a connection.*
>
> (*Rebecca*)

*Chatting doesn't work so you touch him and then that doesn't work then you whisper to him ... Being able to seduce, being able to talk, being able to bullshit. Making them laugh. Every dancer has their own individuality. And some girls do more than others. Sometimes you be bossy and you can get a customer and sometimes sweet and submissive and you can get a customer ... If they're willing to have a laugh and then you have fun with them ... and some don't want you to say anything ... I think I'm more adaptive, I can adapt to people easier now. Once you're in there with all the other girls it's easier to do ... It's like you have the power.*

(*Annelise*)

Deshotels and Forsyth (2006) term this sort of emotion work 'strategic flirting'. Building on Pierce's (1995) concept of 'strategic friendliness', 'where men gain power by manipulating people to comply to their objectives', Deshotels and Forsyth (2006: 235–6) argue that 'dancers orchestrate the sexual fantasies of men to get them to acquiescence to their wishes (give them money)'. The dancers need to be sensitive to the mood that their customers are in and understand the sort of interaction each customer expects or desires from the moment that they meet and manage the interaction so that it is as profitable as possible. In addition this often needs to be carried out in a feminine way (as the workers have mentioned, they must do this while sometimes appearing bossy but most often seductive, friendly, happy caring, sweet and/or submissive).

Interestingly, although many of the workers see these skills as feminine, the dancers did not tend to naturalise these emotional and communication competencies when they were discussed in terms of 'hustling'. For example, this is a skill Rebecca has learned on the job:

*Q: Are the characteristics that make you good at your job related to gender?*

*... I've had the same gender the whole time I've done this but I've got much better at hustling so it's about skills to flirt with people. And you can recognise that same thing in guys but they couldn't do the same job because it doesn't work that way with roles ... So I think the most important thing is that I have a female body.*

Rebecca therefore suggested that strategic flirting is not a competence that stems from biology. However, she suggested that men do not engage in strategic flirting and stripping work because this continues to be a feminine role rather than a masculine one. Unlike men, she can profit from this skill because, once again, she has the right body for the job; she has female capital.

Why is the emotion work that is carried out in nursing and social work naturalised for women more frequently than it is in this occupation? Perhaps this tendency has something to do with the fact that this work involves manipulation and the direct exchange of money (the worker-client relationship is a commercial relationship) and therefore distanced from altruism. In addition, this work is quite often a conscious performance that occurs in a hyper-real environment (the night club) and on a stage or in a show rather than in a community or hospital setting as is the case for the emotion work that is performed by nurses and social workers. In addition, this might also be because this work is not associated with mothering. As this labour involves sexualised inter-actions and men are not in a subordinate position to the emotion worker these emotional competencies are not associated with the mother-child relationship, in fact sexiness is often distanced from mothering.

### Glamour and feminine capital

The hyper-feminine, sexualised bodies and dispositions that are bought and sold and capitalised on by women in high-end strip clubs come together in glamorous performances. Glamour is a key ingredient to the workers' performances in that it legitimates the work environment, the patrons' presence and the workers' labour. This is why these strip clubs are marketed as glamorous and this is why some of the women aspired to this job and anticipated that it would bring empowerment. As Skeggs (1997: 110) argues 'glamour is the mechanism by which the marks of middle-class respectability are transposed onto the sexual body, a way in which recognition of value is achieved'. Glamour, as a facilitator of respectability, is an asset, and here the connection between glamour and empowerment becomes clear. Skeggs states that femininity via glamour operates as:

> a disposition *and* a form of cultural capital, even if only momentarily and always tied to a performance. It is the attitude that makes the difference. ... Glamour is about performance *with* strength. ... Glamour is a way of transforming the banalities of femininity which render women as passive objects, as signs of appearance without agency, as something which has to be done.
>
> (1997: 110–111)

Glamour enables hyper-feminine sexualised bodies and dispositions to not only act as gender capital in that they can be exchanged for economic and social capitals, it also provides feminine bodies and dispositions with respectability.

Moreover, glamour provides empowerment in that it requires a certain attitude, 'it is a 'structure of feeling' (Williams, 1961: 1977)' (Skeggs, 1997: 110), and so it makes women feel good about themselves. This is what Annelise and Eliza were discussing at the beginning of the chapter. Glamour is partly valuable because it provides self-confidence which is relevant to a good life as well as a high-class one. This is important to these workers as these women are struggling to improve their positions through the gender economy – they want to feel valuable because they are women and feminine rather than subordinate because they are women and feminine. As Skeggs (1997: 112) says this is about knowing that their investments in femininity are worthwhile, but more than this, it is about improving their positions in the gender and class orders. It is about being valuable despite being female and working class.

## The parameters of feminine and female privilege

As I stated previously, as with nursing and social work there are limits to the extent to which femininity and femaleness are privileged in this type of work. To start with, glamour is a tenuous avenue for the achievement of self worth. This is because it is dependent on masculine standards of desirability but also because glamour is particularly difficult for working-class women to sustain and may even be regarded as 'degrading' (Pearce, 1995 in Skeggs, 1997: 110) '... unless 'protected' and defended by other marks of middle-class respectability (such as education or wealth)' (Skeggs, 1997: 110), which many of these working-class women do not hold.

In addition, underlying the performances there also often exists many unfavourable aspects to exotic dancers' working conditions. Unlike the men in Pierce's (1995) study that was mentioned above, the exotic dancers I spoke to reported experiencing both empowerment and *disempowerment* through this strategic interaction (and this was also found in Deshotels and Forsyth's 2006 study). In particular, while women may be well equipped for emotion work they do not necessarily find this work easy. For example, some of the dancers I interviewed are uncomfortable with the ethics of their interactions:

*Some girls are good at talking to people in the right way and are able to do that every time. But it makes me cringe sometimes. ... I'm not one of the top girls.*

(Lea)

Other studies on emotion work have also found that women are more uncomfortable with strategic or manipulative interactions than men and it is argued that this may be because manipulation is not an aspect of normative femininity – it 'fits' better with masculinity (Hochschild 1983; Leider 1993; Pierce 1995; Rollins 1985 in Deshotels and Forsyth, 2006).

And, perhaps for this reason, some dancers also find providing a performance that is different to their 'authentic' selves difficult:

*I'm better than before but I'm not very good at it still in terms of putting on this act and persona. Especially compared to some of the other girls. I've seen them just switch like that – like this new persona. ... And all types of performing are different too. Like if I'm totally fine if I'm performing on stage but my biggest problem is performing another personality. I'd actually have to think of what that other personality would say and I can't do that.*

*(Annelise)*

However, it seems that worker-client interactions in strip clubs are not always manipulative, sometimes genuine friendships are formed: *And sometimes you want to hang out with them ... Regulars would try and form a friendship and then I'd say 'let's go out after' (Annelise).* But this can create its own problems as it makes the boundary between work and friendship difficult to discern: *... I'd see them as friends and it would be hard to draw the line ... (Annelise).* Annelise's narrative indicates one of the stresses of emotion work. Emotional distance is difficult to maintain but nonetheless necessary for dancers because they risk 'emotion fatigue' or 'burnout' if they become too close to customers (Hochschild, 1983).

### Emotion fatigue: 'no one likes a miserable stripper'

As McDowell (2009:108) points out, in sex work '... two forms of emotional labour are being undertaken concurrently: emotional labour on the self by workers to protect their integrity and the production of a version of emotional involvement with clients to satisfy their demands for an authentic sexual experience'. Many of the dancers talked about how fatiguing this labour is, particularly the strain of suppressing real emotions in order to perform in a way that will earn money and success within the field:

*If you're in a bad mood about something then it's just the worst place to be ... (laughs)*

*(Eliza)*

*I guess I probably have to act in a different way than I usually do ... I think I'm quite shy ... not always extroverted. And so if I'm tired I find it hard because I have to be bubbly and extroverted.*

(*Kristin*)

Q: *What do you dislike about your job?*

Lea: *...having to pretend to be nice to people. That feels bad, having to be nice to them when you're not feeling good.*

These narratives indicate that sexualised hyper-feminine performances cannot be consistently sustained by most women and so this is not a stable capital. Further, 'not doing gender well' (Mavin and Gandy, 2011) results in diminished economic capital:

*Some nights I don't want to go in. Some nights if I'm in a good mood I can chat to people and also you can drink. And so you feel like you're not at work, just going out and having a drink. And if I have a good night I feel good about earning lots of money. But if have a bad night I feel bad. That's why kept a spreadsheet ... So you can see that it evens out.*

(*Lea*)

Eliza is very aware of the economic pressure to perform; her employer and customers will not be sympathetic if she fails at this:

*If you be there and you're not in the right frame of mind, like a party frame of mind then you're not going to make any money because no one likes a miserable stripper (laughs). ... You have to be happy, people want to have a good time and no one gives a shit if you've got rent to pay (laughs). 'Get another job (laughs)!'*

This work can also lead to a kind of emotional 'burn out' in other aspects of the dancer's lives:

*It* (exotic dancing) *builds your social skills but I'm also really sour to people on the phone and things than I used to be that's the downside.*

(*Annelise*)

Annelise described the cost of what Hochschild (1983: 7) calls becoming an 'instrument of labour'. The strain of the commodification of feeling can lead to injury in the workers' own emotions; when a worker commits all of their positive feelings to their work performances the result can be that positive feeling is depleted in their private lives.

Indeed, Eliza suggested that without resilience this can be a dangerous line of work:

*Confidence is the best characteristic you can have. And being resilient to people. Not taking people too seriously. You've got to have the right ... Lots of girls are a bit unstable in general and you can easily go off the rails.*

Again, this implies that emotional distance is needed for this labour. Eliza does not associate resilience with femininity (like one of the nurses, Christine, did), she associates this quality with working class-ness. For Eliza this resilience is enabled by her working-class habitus:

*Q: Do you find that confidence and resilience easy?*

*I think because I come from a rough background. Like from a working-class area it's easier. I just see it for what it is. But a lot of girls, like the Australian girls have had a better upbringing so they're a bit nicer and they're like 'oh but my daddy told me I'm a princess (laughs).*

Hochschild (1983: 159) supports this characterisation of working-class emotional competence. She argues that lower class parents do not tend to focus on their children's emotions and may teach their children to manage their emotions well (rather than emphasise their importance). This suggests that, especially since almost all of the dancers identified as working class, working-class dispositions may be valuable within this occupation. Perhaps this is an industry where working-class dispositions, in combination with feminine and female capitals, can work as assets.

## Clients and workplaces

Although feminine and female capitals may work to provide women with employment and success in this industry, there are many negative aspects to working in strip clubs. In particular, while clients can provide positive appraisal which leads to confidence and a sense of empowerment as well as access to a lifestyle and social networks (social capital) that these working-class women would not otherwise experience, negative exchanges between dancers and customers appear to be frequent and all of the dancers stated that badly behaved clients are one of the ugliest aspects of this work. 'Emotion drain' is contributed to by clients who can be both rude and dangerous, especially at buck's nights:

*Q: What do you dislike about your job?*

*Lea: When people are rude or disrespectful and just guys being guys because they're drunk grabbing your ass and that sort of thing.*

*I'm really lucky though. Customers have told other girls like 'you're overweight, you're ugly' (Eliza).*

The negative attitudes of the customers also impact many of the dancer's relationships with men outside of the clubs:

> *For some girls the job made them unhuman. ... Men ... you don't resent them but you're less likely to take bullshit. You're not as naive ... You get really negative, 'all men this and that'... but then I worked in pubs for a while and realised it's like they're not all like that ... You forget about the men that aren't in there.*
>
> *(Annelise)*

For Annelise, the emotion drain experienced from strategic flirting and customers' behaviours led to her to quit her job:

> *Q: Why quit?*
>
> *I felt unappreciated – and treated like a phase and treated with lack of respect and feeling unrespected by the customers. ... When someone ignored me I'd get offended. If someone didn't want you to dance for them I'd feel offended. I'm quite sensitive like that. ... Also people* (customers) *you'd meet in that environment or outside would not treat as you a person.*

So while Annelise entered this line of work for attention and to be appreciated for her looks, and while she originally experienced a sense of empowerment, this experience was not sustained. These negative experiences led Annelise to convert to Islam, a religion that promotes modesty and sexual restraint for women:

> *I converted to Islam before I got married. I looked into Islam and then wore the scarf a couple of times and went back to work and took it from there.*

Although Annelise is not alone in her resentment towards disrespectful customers she is the only dancer who quit because of this resentment and interestingly, Annelise is the only dancer who comes from a middle-class background. This might be some evidence in support of Eliza's claim that this is a job where working-class women have a better feel for the game. Alternatively, Annelise may have more resources than the working-class women and therefore less to lose from quitting.

However, dancers' experiences of abusive clients vary from club to club and clubs also vary in their responses to poorly behaved customers:

> *You can get some real dickheads. But it's different. Like, I work for* (club name) *which is a really good club and if I said to the security guard 'I don't like the look of that guy' then he'd kick him out. Whereas in other clubs the customer comes first and so I imagine other girls would put themselves in dangerous situations'.*
>
> *(Eliza)*

In some clubs, laws about the level of sexual interaction are sometimes bent to advantage the clients: *Where we work it's technically illegal but they're not too strict about all the rules. You can be like 'no touching' to some and then not to others ... 'a little bit' (Rebecca).*

Although many of the dancers talked about the appeal of the flexibility in this type of work this also comes at a cost. Many of the participants talked about how they are treated disrespectfully by club owners, as if they are 'dispensable':

> *But in a lot of regards it in an industry you don't have any rights like if you're sick or hurt yourself at work you don't have any rights ... They can fine you for things and if you don't think it is fair then tough luck ... In a newsletter at the club I used to work at they said: 'remember girls, all of you are dispensable' ... At that club the boss would yell and treat you like kids and then when the Grand Prix was on they would get girls from interstate and put up the fee ... I don't work there anymore. And they've got in the contract they can fire you without any reason ... If you miss a podium or if you don't show up and you're late you get a $50–100 fine. I got in a disagreement over a fine and so I left that club.*
>
> *(Lea)*

So it seems that, despite unionisation, these workplaces are not appropriately regulated. All of the dancers discussed the difficulties they have experienced in finding a club where they are not harassed or mismanaged by their employers.

What is more, as indicated earlier, the income from stripping can fluctuate, as it depends on how well each dancer performs and 'hustles' on the night as well as the clientele. The hours are also long and the shifts are, of course, mostly as night. Furthermore 'being your own boss' has it its drawbacks in that if a dancer does not work she does not earn money:

*Sometimes you finish at 8 am, sometimes 3am, and then you don't want to get out of bed till 3pm, so you don't have a life. And you'd try to have a weekend off but all you can think about is the money you're missing out on and you can become a workaholic.*

(*Annelise*)

## Dangerous lifestyles

All of the dancers talked about the dangers of the lifestyle connected to this type of work. For example, Annelise stated that the lifestyle associated with exotic dancing was one of the reasons that she left the job. She stated:

*You have to be careful that you don't fall into drug taking. Cocaine and all those drugs on tables. And you'd see the girls and then they'd do it out in the open.*

Drug taking was mentioned by a number of the workers I spoke with and this, particularly cocaine, is connected with the 'glamorous' and 'expensive' lifestyles of some of their clients, but, as McDowell (2009: 108) argues, drugs may also be a means to cope with the demands of emotion work and to create some emotional distance from their work activities. However, as Annelise acknowledges, this is a dangerous means of emotion management.

Annelise also commented:

*I feel now ... before it was all about ... it was always a competition about who makes the more money and who has better hair and clothes. You always have to get your nails done and buying tans ... There's also hair extensions that need to be fixed and new outfits. So you don't really have a life. But I did get to live in a really nice house ... but all the money went on things ... I wonder where it all went. Eyelashes every few nights ... always forking out ... and you don't want it in your bank because you'll get taxed so you keep it and then you wonder where it went ... My goal would change every week and I only ended up saving $1000. First of all I wanted a house and then the money just went on lifestyle and going out. I got a horse – that was good for me.*

So it seems that the cost and time involved with beauty upkeep, the tendency for dancers to spend their money on expensive lifestyle goods and the ubiquity of drugs and alcohol are all distracting elements of the job for those who are trying to 'get ahead'; performing a high-class lifestyle gets in way of real class mobility. In addition, as Atkinson (2009: 905) argues, the temporal experience of the week being based around the pay packet and short contracts (and in the case of stripping – a fluctuating income) may reinforce a short-term outlook among workers so that their attitude is to 'live for the moment' rather than focus on long term projects like career development, saving and class mobility. This might therefore be another example of how a work environment may impact the habitus.

### Unrespectable dirty work

Exotic dancing is perceived as 'dirty work' (Mavin and Gandy, 2011). Hughes (1958) coined the term dirty work 'to refer to occupations or tasks that are likely to be viewed as undesirable or degrading' (Mavin and Gandy, 2011: 4). All of the dancers appeared to agree with this definition of their occupation in their discussions of the 'unrespectable' status of this work. In particular, many of the workers talked about being judged by others for engaging in sex work and many expressed concern that those outside of the field saw them as immoral. For example, Eliza stated: *It's different because some people think you're like the scum of the earth. Especially people's girlfriends.* For many of the dancers this is the hardest aspect of the job:

> Q: *What do you dislike about your job?*
>
> Kristin: *The social stigma of it. I used to feel really bad about it … like I was a really bad person.*

Here it can be seen that this work has negative implications for the women's identities despite temporal experiences of respectability through glamorous performances. This is because sex work, in general, is socially dishonoured and in this way, as McDowell (2009: 110) comments, sex work is unique:

'The category "sex work", O'Connell Davidson (1995) suggests, is a liminal one which exists 'in a space between two worlds; a space that is incompletely dominated by the free market ideology and incompletely detached from premarket values and codes (shame, dishonour etc.)'.

Eliza suggested that social stigma is more likely to come from the middle class, particularly middle-class women and so is a class issue:

> *I think … I told one girl who was in my masters' class after I finished because I didn't want them to judge me while I was doing it. So I told them*

*and I think she thinks it is a bit weird. She pretends it isn't but I can see that she feels a bit uncomfortable about it.*

*Q: And why do you think she feels uncomfortable?*

*Because she's really middle class. I'm just a new middle-class person (laughs)! But she went to a boarding school and she's got good Queen's English and everything (laughs)!*

Once again Eliza does not seem to see sex work as compatible with middle-class femininity. However, many of the dancers also frame their work as unrespectable. For example, Lea stated that she would be ashamed of herself if this job was a career, rather than a transitory job that facilitated her education and mobility. She stated:

*I will get a normal job when I can do something that I'm interested in ...*

*Q: There is a time limit on dancing isn't there?*

*There is one woman who is 45 ... I know inside myself I would feel like a bit of a failure because I want to achieve other things in other areas ... like I only get money out of this (dancing), I don't get real satisfaction out of it.*

Lea disassociates her identity from this work and claims that it is simply a means to an end. In this way Lea makes it clear that she is upwardly mobile and only temporarily 'dirty'. As Mavin and Gandy (2011: 16) argue she is a 'good girl' in 'dirty work' – she is distancing herself from stigma and repositioning herself favourably.

However, Eliza suggested that the stigma attributed to exotic dancing is unfounded, particularly in the Australian state of NSW where there is a 'no touching' law:

*And lots of people think it's all 'you get groped and all touching' but in NSW there's that thing where there's no touching. So people are like 'oh my god, you get molested for work' but there's none of that ...*

Eliza is therefore struggling to change the meaning of exotic dancing, she is struggling to make it more respectable, but her method is to distance exotic dancing from sex work and this reaffirms the sex industry's status.

## Secret lives

For many of these workers dancing is a 'secret life'. This, in part, is because one of the strategies that dancers use to achieve '... differentiation and emotional distance, as well as to cope with the demands of the work' is to abstain from disclosing their work roles to family, friends and acquaintances (McDowell, 2009: 108). This creation of distance from their work through non-disclosure is partly required because of the social stigma associated with it. For example, Lea commented:

> *There is the risk of people being judgemental so I don't tell people ... I think by not saying that I do this straight away that I'm giving myself a chance not to be judged.*

Even Eliza has not disclosed her occupation to her parents because it seems that she does not want to lower their social status:

> *My mum and dad don't know. Because they were always like 'if you don't think we will like it then don't tell us'. You know they're all happy about 'my daughter being an OT and moving on her own to Australia'. You know, bragging rights.*

Eliza is content with the status that a caring career like occupational therapy provides her family and does not want it to be depleted by her involvement in exotic dancing.

Kristin talked about how this double life is fatiguing:

> *The close friends I have know but I don't tell people I just met but it feels kind of strange and then if it develops into a friendship it's hard to know when to disclose. ... I don't like working there* (at the club) *anymore. I think it's just ... all the things that go along with dancing: alcohol ... that kind of interaction with people. And I find it hard because I don't tell everyone where I work. And I find it exhausting having that secret kind of life.*

As did Annelise:

> *And there was just lie after lie. So you'd meet people and then tell people you meet lies about what you do for a job, and what you do at night. If you want to get to know anyone it's difficult.*

Here it is clear that, as McDowell (2009: 109–10) argues, dancers must take up performances in their everyday lives as well as their workplaces and because both aspects of their lives 'typically are constructed as an emotional performance based on pretence' dancers experience increasing anxiety from their involvement in this labour. However, when they

do disclose, this causes anxiety as well. All of the dancers commented on how divulging their occupation to others usually strains relationships, especially with parents and partners. For example, Annelise commented: ... *Mum was upset because she'd say what about all the 'old men grabbing at you' and you don't respect yourself.*
For Annelise it may also lead to divorce:

> *My husband knows about it* (dancing) *but we don't talk about it. I would have to leave him if I went back to it. We're having lots of problems with his family at the moment and I'm living with my family. I'm over it.*

Therefore the 'dirty' status of the occupation – its association with dishonour and gendered exploitation, strains relationships.

It is not surprising then, that for most of these workers, class mobility means moving out of the occupation. Even if they enjoy dancing, if they seek mobility, this job is not compatible with their future, (clean) middle-class roles:

> *I do really enjoy it* (dancing), *I think I will be sad to not do it anymore but I think it will be pretty reputation threatening if you were actually employed* (in medicine) *and still doing it.*

> *(Rebecca)*

Exotic dancing therefore offers economic capital and sometimes social capital in the form of networks with clients but workers must limit disclosure or risk dishonour in other areas of their lives. Although they may experience temporal respectability through 'glamour' participation in the occupation cannot be sustained if an individual is to take on a permanent middle-class position. What this reveals about this capital, as Coy and Garner (2010: 665) state, is that it is a 'double-edged sword, dancers (just like the glamour models Coy and Garner (2010) studied): '... can acquire economic power through their bodies but in doing so are ultimately denied legitimate social status'.

## Conclusions

In this chapter I have explored the operation of gender, class and gender capital in exotic dancing. I have found that, although many workers have not had long-term ambitions to enter this occupation and have not been encouraged to enter the occupation by family, this is a career choice that appears to offer more rewards than other jobs that are available to working-class women and enables working-class mobility. This career choice is also appealing to women in that it is seen to offer empowerment through sexiness and glamour (which women are possibly socialised to desire). In these ways, taking up this feminised job is a gendered choice but also a classed one.

This chapter has argued that in this occupation 'doing gender well' in the form of a sexualised hyper-femininity is rewarded. I have demonstrated that women's gendered bodies and dispositions, in particular sexualised hyper-feminine bodies and dispositions, are advantageous within the occupation and are traded for economic and social capital (in the form of advantageous social networks with clients). Many of the exotic dancers I interviewed anticipated this advantage when entering the occupation. Women know that within this occupation they will gain employment easily, without an education. What is more all of the workers talked about cultivating sexualised hyper-feminine bodies though beauty regimes and plastic surgery and using common sexual scripts in performances to 'talk', 'care' and 'hustle' their way to success within the occupation. They therefore consciously build on and manipulate this capital. Workers are aware that feminine bodies and competencies enable them to play 'the game' of the occupation and play it well. Moreover, I have argued that dancers who work in high-end clubs partake in glamorous performances which also enable temporal respectability and a sense of empowerment.

Nevertheless, within this chapter I have demonstrated that there are parameters to feminine and female privilege within this occupation. Emotion drain and poor working conditions are of particular concern and the temporal nature of this work as well as the associated lifestyle can distract from class aspirations. In addition, participation in this work requires 'secret lives' and strains relationships with family and friends. In this industry, once again, feminine capitals and female capitals are assets which always operate within constraints. Moreover, the respectability that can be gained from glamorous performances is most probably only fleeting as it reliant on masculine appraisal and is compromised by these other elements of the job and is not necessarily protected by other markers of middle-classness.

The findings suggest that there are significant ways in which exotic dancing is different to social work and nursing so that there is distance between these two types of workers. Most significantly, as Mavin and Gandy (2011) point out, although exotic dancers 'do gender well' their work is still classified as 'dirty'. Exotic dancers are not rewarded for performing gender in the same way as nurses and social workers are. Doing gender well does not make their work 'clean' and honourable or provide sustained respectability.

Nevertheless, exotic dancers are seeking out respectable positions, just as the nurses and social workers are, they are simply doing this through another avenue: through a sexualised hyper-feminine sexualised aesthetic and glamorous performances (but both occupational groups are appealing to gender norms). In addition, exotic dancing may be an occupation where a working-class disposition is an asset (although a middle-class aesthetic may be more profitable). Like nursing and social work, exotic dancing seems to be an occupation where working-class women can achieve mobility.

This chapter also demonstrated how women benefit from their participation in exotic dancing and therefore provides a more nuanced explanation for women's involvement in sex work than one of mere coercion or discrimination. Women *capitalise* on their femininity and femaleness within exotic dancing: they gain temporary respectability and a sense of empowerment as well as a reasonable income which may fund other mobility activities like completing higher education. So I have demonstrated how women actively *contribute* to the feminisation of this work. The concept of 'gender capital' may therefore be useful in overcoming the dichotomy between exploitation and liberation that is found in theoretical work on exotic dancing and sex work more generally. As with Deshotels and Forsyth (2006) and Mavin and Gandy (2011) I argue that exotic dancers are both empowered and disempowered. They wield gender capital, but within limits.

The next chapter examines gender, class and gender capital in hairdressing, another occupation that sells a particular aesthetic.

# 8
# Hairdressing

This final 'case study' chapter looks at gender, class and gender capital in hairdressing. Once again, this is an occupation in which gender capital appears to operate, particularly feminine capital. However, the structure of this capital is more akin to the capitals that are valuable in exotic dancing than in nursing and social work. In addition, as with exotic dancing, working-class people appear to dominate this field and so stories of class mobility and limits are prevalent.

This chapter draws on the voices of the hairdressers I interviewed and occasionally on narratives from Robinson, Hall and Hockey's (2011) study *Masculinities, Sexualities and the Limits of Subversion: Being a Man in Hairdressing*. Within this chapter I look at both male and female workers' experiences of the hairdressing industry and I argue that feminine capital is a resource that is drawn upon by both male and female workers, just as it is in nursing. Once again, I would like to start the chapter with a discussion of 'gender stories' and how choices fall in line with the doxic system and are supported or unsupported by friends and family. I then move on to look at 'class stories', 'gender capital' and then finally discuss 'the parameters of feminine privilege'.

## Gender stories

Gender was significant in the occupational choice process for the hairdressers and for their work experiences and trajectories. For example, when asked about their motivations for pursuing this work, the female hairdressers I spoke with talked less about money and more about creative drive and, like many of the social workers and nurses, they did not consider many alternatives when making their career choices. As with the nurses and social workers, this may be because hairdressing is viewed as a good 'fit' for women; it is associated with femininity because of its focus on aesthetics and servicing others. The male hairdresser I interviewed, in contrast, was motivated by a desire to leave a low-status retail job and earn money and prestige, and his choice appeared to be much more conscious. Adam, unlike the female hairdressers I spoke with, also emphasised his interest in the technical aspects of the work and aligned this interest with his father's:

> *I suppose I'm drawn to anything where I can work and express myself; I suppose those are the things that excite me. And the structure of it excites me; I suppose building things up ... the technical side of it, which I suppose I got from my dad.*

He also talked about his interest in 'problem solving':

> *Well, you're solving problems all day, that's the way I look at it, I'm always looking to make sure people have better looking hair and so forth.*

Adam is differently motivated and also constructed this work in a different way to the female hairdressers within his narrative, he emphasised the aspects of hairdressing labour that are commonly associated with masculinity (technical proficiency and logic) and perhaps by doing this he is actively validating his participation in a feminised occupation. Most of his description could just as easily be applied to construction work as it is to hairdressing. This is not an uncommon process for men in feminised work. In her research on male nurses Ruth Simpson (2004) found 'that men relabel their work as masculine and emphasise the masculine characteristics and distance themselves from women in the workplace. Leidner (1993) also found these sorts of strategies in her study of insurance agents' (cited in McDowell, 2009: 178). In this way, Adam is attempting to make the masculine matter, and therefore change the feminised state of play within the occupation. Furthermore, although Adam is defying the gender order by participating in feminised work, by aligning himself with masculinity in this way he is also reinstating it.

## Maternal worlds

Although none of the hairdressers' mothers were themselves hairdressers, all of the hairdressers' mothers were full time homemakers and so their work is similarly gendered. Moreover, for all of the hairdressers, this is a job that their mothers approved of.

Interestingly, Adam's mother also featured significantly in his discussion of choice. He talked about how supportive she was and also stated:

*Um, I think the fact that I was always social, I think that played a big part in it* (his career choice). *I think the fact that my mother always taught me to respect other people. I think that's been a guiding thing.*

Adam inherited a sociality and a compassion for women from his mother and this influenced his choice. Like many of the female workers I spoke with for this study, he appears to be situated in a 'maternal world'. This illustrates that while it may be mostly girls who take on similar practices and occupy similar positions to their mothers, boys may also live in continuity with their mothers. Once again, the gender order can be transgressed.

### Ordinary gender relations

Despite his discussion of the masculine elements of hairdressing, Adam's decision to pursue hairdressing was met with disapproval from friends and family and assumptions were made about his sexuality. Adam stated that his decision to be a hairdresser confused other young men who he was acquainted with when growing up. These young men assumed he was homosexual rather than heterosexual:

*All the real homophobic guys around where I grew up, I'd keep them guessing – 'I saw him with a different girl', 'so did I – with two different girls' (laughs).*

This assumption may, in part, be because of the association that is made between gay men and aesthetic competence. In addition, just as was the case for the male nurses, because they are transgressing gender norms and are not doing hegemonic masculinity well, it may be assumed that male hairdressers do not do heterosexuality well either.

Adam has never made this assumption about men who work in hairdressing because he was inspired to defy gender norms by his first creative director, a mentor who thoroughly embodied masculine heterosexuality:

*And he was a real rock star hairdresser. ... long blonde hair, beard, open shirt, medallions, big expensive car, all the things ...*

*Q: So he was quite inspiring, at that age?*

*Well, I suppose at that age you see someone like that who's at the peak of his career and is quite sort of um ...*

*Q: And did it help that he was a man?*

*Yeah, yep. And straight as well. Not that that was a problem for me. Especially at that time for being a male hairdresser you got a lot of stick and a lot of abuse and stuff. People give you lip about your sexuality and stuff, you know.*

So it seems that seeing another man maintain his heterosexual masculinity while at the same time taking on a feminised role encouraged Adam to also do gender differently. Adam's mentor demonstrated how masculinity can be maintained while participating in a feminine practice. This is interesting as it gives some indication of how more men might be encouraged to enter the occupation: it might be a more acceptable occupational choice for young men if they could be shown how they might be able to participate and still retain their sense of masculinity.

Adam continues to be subject to assumptions about his sexuality; it is often assumed that he is homosexual:

*Q: Does that (questions about Adam's sexuality) still happen?*

*Adam: Yeah, I think it definitely in the psyche. I mean, I don't think people talk about it so much but ... I mean, just a thing that happened at a wedding the other day would be a typical thing. Like you know, I was at a wedding and I was talking to a girl and then my friend turned up and I didn't introduce her to my friend and 20 minutes later she was saying to someone, 'what is (Adam's) boyfriend's name again?' And my friend was completely affronted but I thought it was hilarious, I wouldn't leave it alone, I was like a terrier with a rat, I was camp all day 'look at you darling!' ... it was so funny ... But it is part of the psyche because say you had just met me and I said I was a hairdresser and you could see I was on my own, you'd probably say 'he's probably gay', you know.*

Moreover, while none of the women's parents disapproved of their career choices, Adam experienced a lack of support from his father. When he was asked how his dad responded to his career choice Adam stated:

*My father just about went into orbit ...*

*Q: So did he have visions of you doing engineering?*

*Adam: Yeah, he did. He wanted me to do it but I you know ...*

*Q: And did he mind it was feminised?*

*Adam: I don't know what he thought. I suppose he did.*

Later in his interview Adam highlighted how all of the men in his family worked in the steel industry, an industry that is aligned with working-class masculinity, and so for Adam's father hairdressing did not 'fit' with this family tradition. Engineering, as a career choice, in contrast to hairdressing, would have reinforced Adam's masculinity and would have been in line with the way in which men do gender in his family. However, as I will discuss later, while Adam's father did want Adam to take up a masculine position, he did not want Adam to reproduce his family's class position (Adam's father aspired for class mobility).

Perhaps as a consequence of these experiences, Adam seemed to defend his masculinity throughout the interview. Although (as I will comment on later) he discussed his femininity, he was also quick to highlight his masculinity to counter this admission:

*I think masculinity and femininity ... both parts are just as important ... but I can be just as male as anyone, with the boys (laughs).*

Adam talked frequently throughout the narrative about his attraction to women, love of soccer and his 'boorish' mentality. It seems it is therefore necessary, if engaging with this work, for men to reinforce gender norms while simultaneously subverting them. This need for men to reassert their masculinity so as not to be imagined as an 'other' was also found in Robinson, Hall and Hockey's (2011: 43) research:

The association of hairdressing with gayness (through everyday assumptions and cultural representations) reveals the tenacity of 'homosexual other' against which men must create a masculine sense of self, even among hairdressers who might feel comfortable with being, or becoming, feminized.

## Class stories

All but one of the hairdressers I talked with claimed to come from working-class backgrounds and occupy working-class positions. Moreover, the class history of the middle-class woman (Stacy) is 'muddy' – although Stacy's parents owned their own home, they lived off one low income in a poor suburb and so were probably lower-middle class at best.

In addition Stacy was like the rest of the hairdressers I interviewed in that she has little educational capital.

Adam and Melissa discussed their limited educational capital and also mentioned that they had little interest in school:

> *Although I was always terrible at school, terrible at it, in wood work classes or metal work classes, I guess I just wasn't very focussed as a student. I was focussed on girls and soccer.*
>
> (*Adam*)
>
> *I didn't do very well at school; I didn't get great grades.*
>
> (*Melissa*)

As with many other working-class people, educational capital was not something that they were encouraged to invest in.

In addition, when they began the occupational choice process the hairdressers did not contemplate middle-class occupations (although as I will discuss shortly, Stacy did briefly study fine arts later in her career), anything other than a working-class job was outside of the realm of possibility for these workers and so they have limited themselves from areas of social life that they are already denied access to (Bourdieu, 1984). As I discussed in Chapter 3, hairdressing is conceptualised as a 'realistic aspiration' for working-class individuals (Sharma and Black, 2001: 916).

However, hairdressing is a respectable working-class occupation; it is not morally compromising like exotic dancing, it requires skill and certification and it provides a fairly reliable source of income. Furthermore, hairdressing is a diverse industry that includes high-status workplaces and so offers the possibility of mobility. For these reasons, for Adam, hairdressing was a better option that a low-skilled retail job:

> *I didn't know what I wanted to do ... I was just working in jeans stores and stuff and all these apprentices would come in and buy clothes and I would see them out on the weekend clubbing and stuff and they would just hang shit on me for working such a dead end job and said I should get work as a hairdresser. So I trawled the whole of the city from one end to the other to see what salons I could find and I ended up getting a job in the best salon in all of Glasgow.*

Adam was therefore trying to improve his position and although hairdressing is also service work, it is not a 'dead end' job in that there is room within the industry for career progression and it is associated with a fashionable lifestyle.

Moreover, as I mentioned previously, hairdressing is more respectable than most retail jobs in that it is skilled and this skill is certified; hairdressing is a 'trade'. It seems that a trade is a particularly respectable career for working-class individuals because a trade is an educated position that provides a stable income but it is also a modest position and training takes place within further education institutions or 'on the job' rather than within universities, which are associated with the middle class; trades are therefore within working-class limits. It might be recalled that one of the social workers, Ruth, in Chapter Six stated that her working-class parents value a trade over a profession and the importance of trades for the working class was brought up by several of the hairdressers as well:

> *My mother was always concerned with me getting a trade, she always wanted me to have a trade. She said 'if you have a trade then you're qualified then you can go anywhere and work, so if there's not work available where you are then you can move somewhere and work'.*

> *(Adam)*

> *Melissa: I mean they said airhostessing wasn't a real career, it is just like glorified waitressing so hairdressing was a better career for me ... more skill.*

> *Q: And what does your partner think?*

> *Melissa: Oh, he thinks it's great that I've got a trade because you can always do it whenever and wherever.*

Within their narratives both Adam and Melissa highlighted how important it is to their family that they have a 'trade' and a 'skill' but also that this trade enables them to work 'anywhere' or 'wherever'. Their parents and partners are conscious that, in the contemporary labour market, it is important for workers to be flexible and this might, in part, be a consequence of deindustrialisation, a phenomenon that most severely impacted working-class communities (McDowell, 2009: 2–3).

However, not all of the hairdressers' parents viewed their career choices in a favourable light. As I stated earlier, Adam's father, who aspired for class mobility, was one parent who disapproved of his son's career choice, and this is not only because of hairdressing's feminine status, but because of its working-class status:

> *he just didn't think very much of the industry and he never knew anyone who was a hairdresser so he was, you know ... He changed his mind when I became successful or minorly successful ...*

*Q: What do you think he didn't like about the industry?*

*Adam: I suppose because my parents are working class, even though my dad did really well and put himself through uni, you know, he had a descent career, he was always trying to get away from his working-class roots and some kind of aspiration for ... to be some sort of middle class ... So I think he probably thought it was the lower end of the spectrum, very working-class people, and he didn't want me spending my time with them.*

This narrative highlights the common understanding of hairdressing as a working-class occupation. Adam's father desired an engineering career for his son and Adam's father hoped that Adam would associate with middle-class people. He had worked hard to achieve mobility and his son was undoing this. It is only when Adam achieved seniority in the industry and his position appeared middle-class, that his father approved of his career choice.

### Limited choice

As has been the case for the other workers, the hairdressers' family members set class limits on their choices. For example, Melissa talked about how her mother pushed her towards this work. Of all the work stories presented in this book, Melissa's appears to be the most influenced by her mother's opinions:

*I wanted to be an air hostess and I wasn't old enough at the time. And my mum said, cause I always did her hair from a young age, even cut it because she's crazy she'd let me cut her hair ... she always said I did a good job but I look back now and it wasn't that good. And she wanted me to be a hairdresser and then my stepdad looked up apprenticeships and he got me an interview at this salon, I started there with intentions of seeing how it went but I ended up really liking it. I had one interview to be an airhostess but I ended up getting there late and so I just stayed with hairdressing. I loved it. Once I started, and you're on such a low wage as an apprentice, you want to stick with it because you don't want to have spent all that time working for peanuts for nothing.*

*Q: And what did your mum like the most about hairdressing?*

*Melissa: Getting her hair done (laughs)! Even when I'm home now my mum changes her hair colour every month and she has it cut, 'oh do you think I just need it thinned a little bit here?' And like when I was home for Christmas I blow dry her hair every two days (laughs). Even if she's in a mood with me she'll sit there waiting with a towel on her head (laughs).*

Melissa's mother therefore limited Melissa's practice. At first, Melissa found it difficult to reflect too much on why her mother pushed her towards this career, except that her skills improve her mother's feminine bodily capital. Later in her interview, Melissa stated that her mum thought that hairdressing was the appropriate place for an artistic daughter:

> *I think she just thought I'd be good at it. Because she didn't push my other sister to hairdressing. I think she knew because I'm artistic and because I'm hands on I'd just love it.*

And hairdressing is certainly a trade that is unlike many others in that it is '... associated with creativity and aesthetics' (Hall et al, 2007: 540). However, while Melissa's mother did not appear to stop her from seeking out higher class pursuits, she certainly did not encourage her to pursue her creativity in any other occupation – hairdressing was the *only* choice, as far as she was concerned. Melissa's story resembles one of the nurse's. It might be recalled from the nursing stories that Tracy stated that while her parents approved of her career as a beautician, they questioned her choice to pursue nursing and it might be speculated that this is because a nurse position is a middle-class one whereas the position of a beauty therapist is a working-class one that fits with a working-class habitus. In both cases the worker's family members are performing symbolic violence – they are limiting the actions of their children so that they fall within class lines.

Stacy, like Melissa was drawn to the creative side of hairdressing. Unlike Melissa Stacy did attempt to explore her creativity via another avenue and left hairdressing briefly to study fine arts but this avenue of study proved to be economically unsustainable:

> *There was no money in it, I couldn't support myself. It's too hard. You're on the dole and then you have to buy all the art supplies. So I left.*
>
> *Q: Why did you leave hairdressing to study art in the first place?*
>
> *Stacy: I finished my apprenticeship but I just got bored of it. I've always loved art so I thought well this is a different side of art, instead of painting people's heads your painting paper. Like I loved it and I wish that I did it until the end but I couldn't pay rent or anything and I thought well ... maybe later on.*

So it seems that hairdressing is a practical alternative for individuals, particularly women, who do not have the resources to pursue other artistic endeavours. It is a trade that allows for some creativity and expression and is located within working-class limits.

However, while Stacy's parents were supportive of her pursuit of a trade, her mother was ambivalent about her ambition to work in the more prestigious parts of the industry:

> *I think for my father ... he didn't mind what I did. I think my parents always drummed into you, you need something behind you to fall back on your feet. So they were very, very supportive. My mum just didn't understand ... but I think she understands now that I just didn't want to work in a suburban shop, I wanted to go further.*

Stacy's mother attempted to limit Stacy's aspirations so they are in line with her class culture, just as Melissa's mother did. She is determining what is 'for' and what is 'not for them'.

## Class mobility

Hairdressing is an industry that contains a diversity of positions. As I discussed in Chapter 3, the differences between shopping centre or suburban salons and inner city 'boutique' salons in terms of status, opportunity and pay is huge; they represent different ends of the hairdressing hierarchy. All of the hairdressers I spoke with work or have worked in trendy inner-city salons that cater for wealthy clients and they are all aiming for mobility of some sort. Stacy and Adam have also worked as trade educators (Adam in top hairdressing academies in London) and both have owned shares in salons at various points in their lives. They have therefore experienced a reasonable amount of success.

Adam discussed how he has always been motivated to succeed within the industry and achieve a high-status position, even when he first began as an apprentice:

> *I was just mad keen because to be the art director's apprentice has all its perks you know, rich clients that tip well for a start plus you get trained by the best stylist in the salon. But all the other apprentices absolutely despised me, but I wasn't there to get along with them, I was there to get on, you know?*

It might also be recalled that Adam desired to emulate a mentor who *was a real rock star hairdresser. ... long blonde hair, beard, open shirt, medallions, big expensive car, all the things ...*

Adam was therefore focussed on success from a young age and sacrificed friendships with his colleagues to achieve this; he consciously strove for mobility. He later commented on the extent to which a hairdressing business can accumulate economic capital and made it clear that this motivates him in his work:

> *The* (multi-national hairdressing company) *family, before they sold the company to an American had so much money, they had their own private jet and* (colleague's name) *used to fly in it sometimes. They'd say 'what time is your flight' and he's say '6 o'clock' and they'd say 'why don't you just come with us?' So there's so many hairdressing salons in the world and so many levels ... there are people in London who charge five hundred quid for a haircut. ... that'd be nice, I could do that (laughs).*

Melissa also has her sights set on mobility. She was quick to emphasis the level of training she received and imagines herself as a celebrity stylist. However, single motherhood has stalled her aspirations:

> *Q: What sort of status (if any) is there to be gained from working in your position and chosen field? How does society reward you for carrying out this work?*
>
> *Melissa: Um ... I don't think they do. Unless you're ... like...I'm watching a lot of those shows ... like the one about that great British hairdresser, James Brown. He's like a high-profile, freelancing hairdresser who is wanted by all the stars. Unless you're something like that I don't think there's much ... you're not thought of as anything.*
>
> *Q: So, like a celebrity hairdresser?*
>
> *Melissa: Yeah. Like I think you'd have to devote your whole entire life if you wanted that. I think anyone could do it but you've got to want it so bad and dedicate everything to it.*
>
> *Q: And that's not something you wanted?*
>
> *Melissa: I always think I would love to do something like that. But I wouldn't now that I have* (child's name). *Like it's a lot of travelling ... I always watch those shows and think 'oh my god, I could do that' and 'oh my god, I could do that!'*

Both Melissa and Adam fantasise about the glamour of celebrity hairdressing. This shows that, although glamour featured in many of the exotic dancers narratives and can have a close relationship with sexualised-femininity, it is not only women who find glamour appealing – for both working-class men and women it appears to be an avenue for escape from the everyday world and to accrue some respectability. In addition, although Melissa is like Adam in that she is similarly motivated, her gender limits her actions; her mothering obligations interfere with her mobility aspirations.

Stacy was also focussed on achieving a high-status position in the industry when she was younger. Stacy's ambition was high-end fashion work:

> *I used to collect ... French Vogue and all those sort of things. And I used to have a scrapbook with pictures of what people do with hair. So I was just really passionate about it. And I think back then I just wanted to ... I didn't want to work in any suburban shop. I was so passionate – I just wanted to get to the top.*

Stacy, like Melissa and Adam, was aiming for success. So it seems that hairdressing is viewed as an avenue for mobility and this may be because it is seen as reasonably meritocratic in that it requires vocational rather than academic training and can enable a high income and access to high-class lifestyles for a limited few.

## Client networks/social capital

Hairdressing may be seen as a gateway for mobility because it can provide a generous income but also because it can provide access to wealthy customers. Hairstyles are an important bodily marker of status and so are particularly significant for class distinction; as Gimlin (1996: 524) remarks, beauty 'is simply one tool women use as they make claims to particular social statuses'. This means that the higher classes are particularly invested in hair styling. Affluent customers also frequent the boutique salons that the hairdressers I spoke with are, or have been, employed in. This job is therefore like exotic dancing in that it provides workers with access to people who they would not otherwise meet, it allows for contact with individuals who are from middle- and upper-class cultures, and therefore potentially expands their social networks outside of their class group and this provides a sense of mobility.

This is commented on by Adam who stated that the social connections he makes are a perk of the job:

> *plus the array of people I get to meet that I wouldn't get to meet in any other profession. I meet professional women, some are mothers, housewives. Plus I get to meet bankers, who I would get to meet otherwise, doctors or ... a whole array.*

Adam elaborated on this later in the interview:

> *Q: What sort of status (if any) is there to be gained from working in your position and chosen field?*
>
> *Adam: You make relationships with people you wouldn't usually make them with and sometimes you become friends. And sometimes they're people you'd never had met in a million years, maybe because of their job or ... they might live somewhere really posh where you'd never ... That's really interesting, that's really fascinating.*

Hairdressing may therefore provide beneficial social connections or social capital. Adam also sees his status as improved by his association with affluent others and for him, this is a drawcard for this type of work. Perhaps, even if he is not in a high status position, he may reach a high status by association.

## Gender capital

Femininity and feminine bodies seem to be highly valued in this industry, just as they are in the other feminised occupations. Hairdressing is thoroughly feminised as it consists of mostly female workers and female clients. What is more, when getting their haircut, the aim for many female clients is to maintain or produce a feminine aesthetic and the workers often embody this too through fashion and hairstyles. As McDowell (2009: 89) comments, this is an environment where, for the most part, '... the joint endeavours of the female worker and the female customers reproduce as near as is possible an idealized image of hegemonic femininity' (McDowell, 2009: 89). Finally, the hair salon is often portrayed in film and common understandings as a place where female friendships and feminine sociality takes place, and this depiction is reinforced by the hairdressers' narratives. As Barber states:

> The hair salon is a space in which women create bonds and form friendships with each other. The relationships emerge out of 'women's talk' (Alexander 2003) and touch (Furman 1997), which are both implicated in the care work performed by women beauty workers.
>
> (2008)

This section of the chapter will talk about this valorisation of femininity and femaleness in the industry in terms of 'gender capital'.

## Feminine bodily aesthetics

All of the hairdressers I interviewed, like the exotic dancers, are attractive and well groomed. The women in particular talked about the significance of fashioning their bodies so that they are as attractive as they can be and therefore more feminine. It is expected they a embody high-fashion femininity and it is intended that this communicates something about the gender and class of the worker but also the trendy salons they work in: that the worker and the salon both do gender and class 'right':

> *I mostly just kept it black clothes and some ... odd things to make it more fashionable. You have to be quite fashionable. ... you have to have your hair done. You can't wear it up, if it's up then it has to be a style. Because when clients walk in you want them to want to have hair like you. It's like an advert for yourself if your hair looks nice. You wouldn't like to have your hair done by someone who's hair is all greasy and swept back. It's like you're a model.*

> (*Melissa*)

So, as McDowell comments, in hairdressing:

> Although ... workers present a non-sexualised appearance, they must also conform to norms of heterosexual attractiveness, wearing visible make up, for example, and having a neat but flattering hairstyle. They must continually work on their own bodies, as well as their clients, to meet these expectations.

> (2009: 188)

This is because the right 'look' is necessary to acquire and maintain clients. Like a lot of other service workers, particularly those in retail, hairdressers 'model' the highly gendered and classed product they sell so that their embodiments are part of the service. Embodiments of beauty and fashion therefore act as capital in this industry and are traded for economic capital. In particular, it seems that, because salons are feminised spaces, female bodies, especially those that embody or perform high-fashion femininity, are a valuable currency. The working-class women's knowledge of this, just like the exotic dancer's knowledge of the value of feminine embodiments, is not something that was predicted by Bourdieu, but, these embodiments may provide women with some status both inside and outside the occupation (especially since they are high-fashion).

## Camping it up

Robinson, Hall and Hockey (2011: 42) find that conversations in hairdressing salons tend to be 'feminised', in that discussion topics include 'food, body shape, diets and local gossip'. Indeed, one of Robinson, Hall and Hockey's (2011: 41) male hairdresser respondents claimed there is only room for femininity in this job:

> *If you saw me doing shampoo and set, giving all this, you just can't do it, you can't be a butch hairdresser, there's no such thing. You can drink and womanise as much as you want at the end of the day basically, when you're working, you are feminine.*

While many men do embody femininity regardless of their occupation, Robinson et al. (2011) argue that within hairdressing the adoption of femininity may also be the effect of working with women and it may allow men to 'fit' the hairdressing culture. If this is the case then I would argue that perhaps men's habituses are impacted by this occupation. This is another example of Bourdieu's 'occupational effects' (Bourdieu, 1987: 4 cited in Atkinson, 2009: 904); the 'spatio-temporal and organizational structure' of forms of work can impact a person's disposition (Atkinson, 2009: 904).

It may also be that feminine modes of being are assets in this industry and men therefore cultivate and wield feminine dispositions to get ahead. Adam discussed his own experiences of 'doing femininity'. He spent some time discussing how important it is that each individual has both feminine and masculine characteristics and how important femininity is in particular. He also mentioned how he performs an effeminate disposition ('camping it up') and discussed how his knowledge of women is superior to other men's:

> *I was just really effeminate that day, just really camp; 'camping it up'.*

> *Q: Do you 'camp it up'?*

> *Adam: I was talking to this girl, a client, the other morning who has mad cork-screw hair, so heavy. And she said I just have to get it cut but my husband wants me to grow it. And I said men are always going on about long hair but men know nothing about hair and even less about women and she burst out laughing. But it's true, men know nothing about women, they have all these skewed ideas of what women are all about, what women's sexuality is all about, and it's certainly nothing to do with hair.*

*Q: So does it give you some insight into women, working in a salon?*

*Adam: Yeah, it hasn't helped me in my relationships though. I relate to women really easily though. Well, I'm working with women all day, you know. Senior stylists, apprentices, the whole gamut.*

Adam chose to describe his behaviour as 'camp' rather than feminine, perhaps to emphasise that he is a man doing femininity. Nevertheless, Adam sets himself apart from other men and is therefore doing gender differently. Adam is not constrained by hegemonic masculinity and the practices it entails. This improves the way he relates to female clients, gives him insights into styling women's hair, but also their sexuality. This helps Adam recruit female clients but once again, confuses others about his sexuality, including gay men:

*Q: Does your femininity help you get clients?*

*Adam: Oh yeah, most of my clients are female. It's funny, I just started working with this gay man, mid thirties and I think he thought I was gay. Because I don't have ... I'm not uncomfortable with people and their sexuality. Sexuality, colour, race, anything, whatever, I just don't really care, I'm open in that way and I think he thought I was gay as well. Cause then I mentioned something about my ex* (woman's name) *and I just saw his eyes going like that (makes big circular motions)!*

Although, Adam's disposition causes some confusion in regards to Adam's sexuality, Adam uses feminine capital in order to work successfully with women clients and women stylists and apprentices. Therefore, for male hairdressers 'becoming more 'feminized' is largely seen as a *positive* thing'; 'the ability to relate to women, as both clients and colleagues, enables men to be better hairdressers' (Robinson, Hall and Hockey, 2011: 41) and accrue economic capital. McDowell (2000: 20) argues that many men might find interactive body work 'unmasculine and demeaning', however, Adam demonstrates that it is possible for men to perform femininity in a way that assists them in their work life and provides them with some satisfaction. Indeed, once again, as Adkins (2005) and Adkins and Lury (1999) suggest, doing femininity may provide men with greater occupational rewards than women.

Furthermore, Adam's example shows how men can do femininity and do it differently. A 'camp' disposition is effeminate; while it may be associated with homosexuality, it may be experienced as less disconnecting from masculinity because of its association with male bodies. In addition 'campness' may be profitable because gay men are seen as particularly skilled at all manner of aesthetic styling. These assumptions are evident in the creation of popular television shows like 'Queer Eye for the Straight Guy' and 'Gok's Fashion Fix' and camp hairdressers may trade in on these assumptions in order to attract and maintain more customers.

## Emotional competence and caring dispositions

One aspect to these 'camp' or feminine performances is a caring demeanour. All of the hairdressers talked about the significance of caring and empathetic dispositions for the job. This is because the hairdressing salon is a site where clients tend to not only have their hair treated and cut, but also engage in intimate discussion:

> *people tell you amazing things. Sometimes things that they wouldn't tell anyone else, things that even their doctor wouldn't know about. Some people don't talk though ... I just have to plug them to death to get it out of them (laughs). ... maybe we're not counsellors but we're certainly an ear, someone who can exfoliate the soul, if there's something that's bugging them they can certainly get it out, you know. ... they talk about it and then they're working through it.*

(Adam)

And these intimate conversations need to be handled with sensitivity:

> *I think in this industry you have to be compassionate because there's so many things people are going through*

(Stacy)

The hairdressers I interviewed, just like Sharma and Black's (2001: 913) beauty therapist interviewees, 'saw their work less in terms of what it does to make women *look* better, more in terms of what it does to make women *feel* better'. They defined their job 'in terms of work with *feelings* as well as the *body*' (Sharma and Black, 2001: 915). Therefore, hairdressers like the nurses, social workers and exotic dancers, engage in emotion work.

Emotional competence is necessary to handle the sensitive discussions that take place in hairdressing salons. However, emotional competence is also necessary because hairdressers are working on transforming an aspect of their clients' bodies – they need to be emotionally sensitive in 'handling the emotional impact of the gap between expectations or ideals and real possibilities' (Sharma and Black, 2001: 929). As Adam stated:

> *I do think that hairdressers should be the gatekeeper between people having really good hair and people really trashing hair and saying 'this has to*

*stop here' because this is not going to go much further the way it is, it's going to start breaking off or falling out. Because people think that hair will always be there.*

Emotional competence is necessary for any kind of work that involves direct contact with human bodies. In this way, hairdressing work is similar to many 'caring' health professions. As Sharma and Black argue:

Emotional labour is precisely what we should expect to be required of any group of workers who 'process' other people's bodies. The more intimate the contact with the body, the more sensitive handling of emotions is likely to be a consideration. It is the failure to do this that is the substance of much critique of doctors. It is the capacity to do this which is such an important part of the professional image of the nurse (Smith 1992).

(2001: 925)

Melissa prides herself on being particularly good at this aspect of the work and despairs that others are not as competent at prioritising clients' emotional needs:

*I learned in the UK that if a client asks you a question about yourself then you always turn that conversation back around so that it's about the client again, it's their time, their money and they're there to feel good, it's not about you. But some people here seem to talk about their nights out, their holidays, and I wouldn't do that. But I'm not like that anyway, not showy like that.*

The hairdressers also discussed how engagement in emotion work can be enjoyable. For example, for Melissa this is one of the most pleasurable aspects of her work:

*I like the way you can change someone's appearance within a couple of hours, you can make them feel good. Someone might walk in feeling really down and walk out feeling really happy. You become like friends with them but not like a real friend, just someone they can tell everything to. I remember even guys would come in for a haircut and spill out everything and some of them don't even need it cut much they just like talking.*

*Q: And you like that aspect of it?*

*Melissa: Yeah. Cause you just kind of, when you go to work you forget everything because you don't talk about yourself, you just talk about other people.*

Now that she no longer strives to work in high-end fashion Stacy also appreciates the rewarding aspects of emotion work:

*Now I'm just happy when people walk out happy. For me, I'm satisfied with seeing happy clients.*

In addition, Adam expressed satisfaction with the interpersonal elements of his work, arguing that he finds it enlightening:

*Plus it's really social. ... I plug my clients for information often. I found out who their married to, how many times they've been married, how many kids they have, if they're educated, everything about them ...*

*Q: And you like that aspect of it?*

*I think you just hear the best stories. We have a human condition where we judge books by their cover without knowing anything about them ... how often would you get to spend so much time with people you don't even know and you find out things about them that you wouldn't have even thought.*

Sharma and Black (2001: 926) suggest that there are several reasons beauty therapists might provide positive accounts of emotion work. Two of these reasons pertain to hairdressers. First, hairdressing is not as standardised as other service work (such as flight attendance); the hairdresser delivers their own personal style of service. Second, hairdressers do not appear to remain in the employment of one salon for long. Many convert to freelance work or combine freelance work with salon work, or set up their own salon and some may combine salon with teaching work. Hairdressers therefore need to be something like an entrepreneur and build up a clientele who will follow them from one place of work to the next. Sharma and Black (2001: 928) argue that this means that the worker '... must take a high degree of responsibility for monitoring her own performance as an emotional labourer'; they are self-governing. Hairdressers might have to perform for clients but they are free to choose how they do this; they express creativity and agency in their work.

As was the case for the other occupations I have researched, the hairdressers articulated emotional competence as a feminine skill. For example, Melissa naturalised emotion skills as feminine skills:

*I'm a good listener ... you have to be a good listener with hairdressing. I always found that I'd quickly build up a strong clientele in salons because*

*I'm a good listener. Because if you listen to your clients they always come back but if you do something wrong then they're gone so you always need to listen to what they want. ... it's crazy, you think people wouldn't make those mistakes but they do. ... everyone visualises things totally different so you have to be sure.*

*Q: So are these characteristics related to gender?*

*Melissa: Listening – yeah! Do men listen? Not really, do they. But I guess if they really wanted to.*

Therefore, it seems that emotional competence is aligned with femininity and an emotionally caring disposition is a 'feminine capital'. Melissa, as with the participants in Gimlin's (1996: 516) study, also claimed 'a self-sacrificing, nearly maternal attachment' to her clients. Gimlin (1996: 516) observes that her female interviewees '... say that they often deny their own wishes in favour of their customers' requests; they make these sacrifices not because of their financial dependence or lower social status but because they care for their clients' (Gimlin, 1996: 516). Again, 'caring about' someone involves prioritising their emotions above your own, this is altruistic work and altruism is associated with 'good' femininity.

However, Adam emphasised his emotional caring skills in his narrative too, and the men in Robinson, Hall and Hockey's (2011: 43) study also commented on taking part in 'care work' on the job. Yet Adam appeared to agree with Melissa in that he defined these skills as feminine rather than masculine. He also remarked that he is unusual in that he is comfortable with the feminine side of his personality. Therefore, gendered assumptions about emotional competence may limit men's entrance into this feminised occupation and provide women with a better sense of fit within this work environment.

In addition, the naturalisation of aesthetic and emotional competencies for women may mean that women are preferred for this work by employers and men may need to work harder in salons to demonstrate that they are just as capable as women. One of the interviewees in Robinson, Hall and Hockey (2011: 39) commented:

*I think it kind of made me work a bit harder. I've always got on with women better, but really, as soon as I got into hairdressing, I think I realized that yeah, okay, I've got to fight a little bit. It's predominantly a female environment ... I think you need to work a little bit harder.*

Robinson, Hall and Hockey's (2011: 39) interviewee also stated that even if there were as many men as women working in his salon, women still dominate:

> ... *(t)he women would be just slightly above us ... they can be quite strong characters.*

Women therefore have an advantage in this industry. There is a hierarchy within workplaces and women wield a certain amount of power because they are seen to be naturally capable in this work. Aesthetic and emotional competence is seen as feminine and femininity is associated with female bodies.

## The parameters of feminine privilege

### Emotional drain

Emotional work appears to bring a high level of satisfaction but it also brings stress (Sharma and Black, 2001: 926). For the hairdressers, like the exotic dancers, this emotional work can be fatiguing. This means that this is not necessarily easy for men *or* women:

> *because it's so emotionally draining ... really emotionally draining. I had shares in the business you know, and I was working 24/7 and taking on everything and clients want to tell you every aspect ... And cause we're like doctors, I mean we're one of the only industries where people watch you work all the time. And people ... you're always touching them and they're touching you and we're like doctors because they tell you all they're problems and sometimes it's like, 'I can't hear any more!'*

> *Q: You're on show a lot of the time?*

> *Stacy: Oh definitely. And if you talk to* (colleague's name) *he may feel differently but because I have children I'm ... my priorities have changed. He loves all that but I can't give what I gave before. I think when I had my shares I had an emotional breakdown and I was just crying at work all the time because I had so much going on. ... and I shut down. I thought 'that's it, I can't take on ...' because people want to tell you everything and you just get overloaded with information and just their emotions and it's just too much ... ... and it's so draining when people touch you all the time.*

*Q: Is it the clients or the people you work with?*

*Stacy: Both. And you can feel their emotions and it's just like, 'don't touch me!' I'm sure if you asked a doctor too they would say the same thing. ... it's like, one of the girls touches me all the time and she's got so much going on and it's like get into your own space! It sounds really negative but you feel it all the time.*

Here Stacy talked about the extent that emotion work can tax an individual. Stacy also commented on how this is bodily labour in that her body is on show and easily accessed by clients, and this can be confronting. This work, like exotic dancing, therefore requires that hairdressers monitor their own emotions as well as the emotions of others. And Stacy reached a point where she felt she could not do this anymore. Her experience demonstrates the price of the commercialisation of labour.

Stacy also commented that as a mother she finds the job *more* difficult, she cannot give the emotional input that she used to, whereas her male colleague who does not have a family finds this aspect of the job more enjoyable as emotion work is not demanded of him at home. This is an interesting point because it seems to contradict the connections made between paid caring skills and mothering. Many of the other women I interviewed in nursing and social work suggested that they are more competent at this work *because* they have children rather than in spite of them.

However, Adam, who does not have any children, also experiences the strain of emotion work:

*Exhausting. After a day at the salon I'm just wiped out. We were talking about that on the weekend because Saturday was such a big day and (colleague's name) said 'I just can't be bothered going out, I think I'll just sit somewhere quietly ...*

Hence, although the hairdressers claimed to enjoy this work in other parts of their narratives, it is nevertheless difficult. Moreover, as with the exotic dancers, the hairdressers frequently talked about how emotion work necessitates performance. For example Stacy commented:

*You know you're always on show so I guess you have some types of ... depends on what kind of client you know. There's a bit of a performance you know, of what they expect. ... I think you have to be happy or fun. It depends on what kind of person you're dealing with, what kind of personality they are.*

Stacy mentioned how being watched by clients while she works intensifies emotion work and this is an issue that came up in Melissa's narrative as well:

> Q: *Do you have to behave in a certain way because you participate in this occupation?*
>
> Melissa: *Yes. Very professional and everything could happen to you on the outside but as soon as you get into a salon you just need to put on a brave face and forget about yourself because it's not about you. Cheerful, happy and even if you disagree with someone you can't let them know ... you can't show it. Even if it's someone you're working with you can't show it because salons are such small spaces and clients can see you. ... you're on show. You don't realise ... cause there's mirrors everywhere, every little face ... and if you say anything they can see.*
>
> Q: *Is this easy for you?*
>
> Melissa: *Sometimes not (laughs). Because people can read what I'm feeling on my face. So sometimes it's very hard for me sometimes to ... But I've got a lot of patience so I can ... but it's quite hard.*

Therefore, hairdressing, like exotic dancing is carried out on stage and this heightens the difficulty of emotion work. It is rare that these workers have a minute to themselves and this means that they must regulate 'every little face'.

Furthermore, the stress of emotion work is also heightened for workers because every hairdresser's livelihood is dependent on their efficacy at it. As Gimlin (1996: 517) comments, 'Hairdressers' financial dependence on customers shapes their willingness to meet emotional needs' and, despite being 'gatekeepers' as Adam commented, and having emotional talents, hairdressers need to defer to customer's hairstyling requests. And this means, that they are 'generally speaking, more like service workers than professionals or artists because their jobs depend in large part in their skill in forging emotional ties with their clients' (Gimlin, 1996: 517).

Emotion work may be straining but it is also viewed as status building; the hairdressers highlighted this labour in order to emphasise the significance of their jobs. Sharma and Black discovered this tendency in their interviewees' narratives too:

> ... the therapists we interviewed were aware of negative images of the beauty therapist (as bimbo, as colluding with the oppression of women, as only having trivial skills and performing trivial work),

and their stress on working with feelings could be a strategy to place their work in a more serious light.

(2001: 921)

In particular, when discussing emotion work, the hairdressers I spoke with referenced the parallels between the roles of hairdressers and doctors, who are professionals who deal with emotions. For example:

> *And you can feel their emotions and it's just like ... don't touch me! I'm sure if you asked a doctor too they would say the same thing.*
>
> (*Stacy*)

> *Sometimes things that they wouldn't tell anyone else, things that even their doctor wouldn't know about*
>
> (*Adam*)

However, as Gimlin (1996) points out, their professionalism may also be undermined because the job requires that workers self-sacrifice and defer to the clients' wishes:

> By providing for their clients emotionally, beauticians *both* support and undermine their own identity claims. On the one hand, by becoming their customers' confidantes and advisers, hairdressers are able to imagine themselves their clients friends' and, by implication, their equals. And seeing themselves as filling the same purpose as therapists, stylists could again find support for their claims to professional status. At the same time, however, because the beauticians imagine themselves as devoted friends, they are forced to put their patrons' hair styling wishes before their own.
>
> (Gimlin, 1996: 524–5).

Furthermore, just as is the case for nursing and social work, the elision between emotion work and femininity means that emotional labour is undervalued. This means that making emotion work visible is not necessarily a useful tactic for raising the status of the occupation. As Sharma and Black argue:

> ... this could be seen as a risky strategy; if emotion work is based on skills which most women automatically acquire through life experience then this (taken on its own at least) provides a shaky basis for claims to recognition and legitimacy.
>
> (2001: 929)

### Austerity trumps femininity

Although they are mostly feminised, salons do differ in their cultures and interestingly, the most affluent salons require that the stylists display as little personality as possible:

> *I think one of the funny things at Sassoons was how austere everyone looked, there were a few flowery kind of personalities but mostly everyone had short hair and even if they were wearing a label it would be the plainest piece from that label ... if you saw them walking down the street you'd probably think that they were an accountant, a trendy accountant. You could be wearing some fabulous label but it'd be really plain.*
>
> (*Adam*)

This austere attitude also extends to the verbal interaction in high-class salons:

> *Our salon is a little more relaxed I guess than some of the other salons. I'm sure in some of the higher class ones you have to show no emotion and ... people pay three hundred and fifty bucks for a haircut. There's a guy in New York that charges one thousand dollars. But women pay it. And for that money they expect that you perform.*
>
> (*Stacy*)

Hence, in the most prestigious workplaces emotion work seems be part of the job but the labour is in limiting the worker's emotions rather than exhibiting care towards the clients. This may mean that feminine dispositions and performances are not as valuable in high-end salons. As with nursing and social work, femininity may assist at the job's entrance level but it is a capital that has limited use in high-status positions.

### Poor wages and working conditions

As with many other feminised occupations that involve interactive body work, hairdressing is poorly paid and usually provides little social status. For example, Melissa commented on how little she earned when she first moved to Australia from the UK:

> *I look back on my wage slip now and I would never settle for that. I think I was on seventeen dollars an hour. I would get out at 9pm at night and I would start at 10am Monday to Saturday and I'd get one day off during the week and I would earn six hundred dollars per week.*

The work is also inflexible and the hours are long. For this reason, the two hairdressers I spoke with who are mothers discussed how salon work is not sustainable while they have small children. Instead, they have now taken up freelance work but this is much less reliable and neither hairdresser is sure of what her wage will be from one week to the next. As a result of this instability Stacy is unsure whether she is now in a better position than her parents:

> *Q: So did it put you in a better position than your parents?*
>
> *Stacy: ... in some ways yes and some ways no. But I think in the 21st century it's really hard for young people to buy property. And I should have bought property back then. But I had shares in the business where my parents didn't and I got to travel so I was a bit more worldly.*

The poor working conditions in salons have also resulted in all of these hairdressers 'opting out' of their careers at certain points, sometimes for a considerable period of time. This is not uncommon. For example, in Australia there are many qualified hairdressers who are working in alternative roles. In 2006 '... of the 125 537 people qualified as hairdressers, at least 43 000 were working as intermediate production and transport workers, elementary clerical, sales and service workers or labourers; and only 34 958 were employed as hairdressers' (DEEWR, 2009: 18).

## Poor status

All of the hairdressers spoke of their awareness of the low status of their jobs. The male hairdresser in particular talked of ways in which training practices and salon environments could be improved to elevate hairdressing to professional status. Adam also often tried to disrupt common assumptions about the significance of the work during his narrative:

> *listening to stories of people that travel to teach and you go on a plane with a business man and he knows you're a hairdresser and he says 'so you're going on holiday are you?'. And you say, 'no I'm going to work' and he'll say 'what, to cut a friend's hair?' So they have no idea at all. I think that what happens is ... there is a certain elitism. Businessmen can't imagine that anyone outside of the business sector would travel for work. Like (colleagues name) travels to LA for (multinational hairdressing company) and people just can't believe that he's flying business class.*

In addition, Adam talked about how salons should be paired back so that there is more focus on the craft rather than the interior of the salon:

> *if I look at hairdressing salons I like them to be really, really plain, I hate those salons with guild frames and all that sort of stuff going on because I don't think you really see the work. The most important thing in a salon should be the work, you should be able to see the hair, but you're in those sort of salons with all those sorts of things and you can't see the work. I think the work should be the expression of the salon, it shouldn't be the decor.*

Adam seems to be pushing for salons to be presented as focussed on skill rather than fashion. Interestingly, this is not as evident in the women's narratives but this may be partly because the environment that he would prefer is also less feminine: in his vision salons are less gendered and this might mean that femininity is less valuable which is not necessarily in the best interests of the women. Adam might be attempting to change the state of play within the occupational space.

## Age limits

Hairdressing, particularly hairdressing in boutique salons and high-end fashion is dominated by the young, just as exotic dancing is. This may be because beauty and fashion are associated with youth. As Alvesson (1991: 997) comments, fashion sense and trend awareness are 'seen as inconsistent with aging'. In addition, this may also be a youthful industry because of the difficult, often physically demanding, working conditions (for example hairdressers must be on their feet for the most part of their shifts). Therefore Stacy, who is approaching 40, is thinking about moving into further education teaching:

> *Q: Why did you decide to have a career change?*
>
> *Stacy: I always wanted to change my career but now that I've worked in the industry so long it's hard. ... I think ... I don't want to be a hairdresser forever. It's a young person's industry and I think it is too many hours and on your feet.*

## Masculine and male capitals

Interestingly the female hairdressers I spoke with do not see the industry as particularly feminised – they noted how it is, for the most part, just as easy for men to participate in the occupation as women. However, this might be a reflection of the workplaces in which they are situated – they all work or have worked in urban boutique and high-fashion salons. These sites are the more prestigious locations for hairdressers and are therefore more likely to attract men.

All of the hairdressers discussed how men now dominate the top positions in their industry and commented that their bosses have often been men. It seems that in hairdressing, like nursing and social work, men achieve the most success. For example, when asked about the prestigious positions in her work Melissa responded:

> *I think it's mostly men that get that high. But maybe it's because they've got more determination ... I don't know. Men always get to high places don't they? So if they're going to be a hairdresser they're going to be the best of the best and up there with the celebs and ... I generally do think men get higher.*

So men dominate the prestigious positions, if women get to the top it is the exception rather than the rule. Melissa commented on how James Brown has achieved celebrity status without a high-fashion bodily aesthetic and so male capital appears to trump the feminine capitals that are valued in the industry:

> *Q: And why don't you think women do that?*
>
> *Women do but ... Even men invented GHD and ... it's always men isn't it. ... but there are some big name hairdresser over here aren't there ... Jayne Wild ... I don't know many but ... ... but James Brown is just this short little guy, no fashion ... well he thinks he has fashion sense and curly, crazy hair and he's now got his own TV show. And he's got a shampoo out ... everything.*

It also seems that clients may prefer male hairdressers. One of Robinson, Hall and Hockey's (2011: 40) male hairdresser interviewees stated 'that many women preferred a man to do their hair because they believed they were *'getting something special'*. This view was confirmed by his female colleagues who reported many women clients wanting a man because they believed that a man was perhaps more skilful'. Assumptions about the superiority of male hairdressing skills may be made because haircutting is, in part, a technical practice and men are often aligned with rationality. However, it may also be that, once again, men's feminine skills are seen as cultivated rather than natural and therefore men's labour is more likely to be recognised. Once again, male workers have more control over the effect that they have on their clients.

Robinson, Hall and Hockey's (2011) respondent and his colleagues also 'described the importance that many women seem to place on receiving flattery and attention from a man' (Robinson, Hall and Hockey, 2011: 40). Similarly, Melissa acknowledged female clients' preferences for men:

Q: *Did your gender assist you in gaining employment within this area?*

*Not really. Cause there's lots of men hairdressers. I think now its fine ... because I think women love having men cut their hair so men are employed just as much.*

This situation is very different to the situation in nursing and social work where female clients and patients tend to prefer to be treated by women.

Furthermore, the male hairdresser I spoke with seemed to be the most accomplished and Adam also talked in some detail about how his gender has personally advantaged him in the industry:

Q: *Did your gender assist you in gaining employment within this area?*

*Adam: Oh definitely. ... I don't really see why women should be treated the same way and paid the same rate. Although we do all get paid the same rate in there* (his current salon).

Here Adam pointed to how women are discriminated against in the industry despite its feminisation. According to Adam women are paid less than men and are not treated equally. Once again, this may be in part, because their labour is less visible. Adam also suggested that a masculine disposition may be valuable in seeking out senior positions:

Q: *So are there any other advantages to being male?*

*Adam: Maybe we're more bullish. Just because men are, you know. And pushier, a bit more aggressive to get in a better position. And not being intimidated, I'm not really intimidated. ...*

Q: *Are the characteristics which make/will make you good at your job related to gender?*

*Adam: I think, planning, I think I plan things. I don't know if that's gender or if it relates to my family, maybe my dad, you know ... he's pretty meticulous, to go from a working-class background to put himself through college and that was when my sister was just a little baby so I think that would've been really, really hard and that might have something to do with it, I don't know.*

While performing femininity may enable Adam to relate to clients and co-workers and recruit clients, his maleness and his masculine dispositions are what helped him push to the top of the hairdressing hierarchy. His comments suggest that in hairdressing, in senior positions and in treatment and in pay, male bodies and masculine capital trump female bodies and feminine capital.

## The parameters of masculine and male privilege

Nevertheless, as the findings in regard to the value of feminine capital indicate, most men must dip in and out of masculine *and* feminine dispositions if they are to succeed. In fact, Adam's masculine habits contributed to the end of his career in a successful London academy:

*Q: So are there any other advantages to being male?*

*Adam: ...maybe that was my problem at* (a prestigious hairdressing academy) *though, I wasn't really intimidated by any art directors or management because I had had so much experience before I got there and then once I was trained and could cut hair as well as them then I wasn't intimidated at all.*

*Q: So you decided to leave then?*

*Adam: Well, maybe I'm a bit more of a handful than others because I'm not going to roll over, 'right away governor', I'm always going to challenge that and say I don't agree with that ... I'm cantankerous and Scottish.*

Adam therefore blames the end of his career in this particular academy on his masculinity and cultural background. In particular, it seems that his working-class masculinity may have held him back in this situation. While other aspects of his narrative evidenced that men can embrace the attitudes that are required for service work, this part of his narrative suggests that his masculinity prevents him from displaying the servility that is also necessary to succeed in this kind of job (just as McDowell (2000: 205) suggests).

Finally, high-status positions in the hairdressing industry are still very rare. Masculine capital and male capital will still not necessarily provide men in this occupation with a high amount of economic capital or prestige.

## Conclusions

In this chapter I have found that hairdressing's working-class, feminine identity makes it the only career choice for many working-class women. In particular, it is considered within reach for women who have artistic competence. Nevertheless, high-status and celebrity positions do exist within this industry and this is why all of the hairdressers I spoke with have hopes for mobility; they are in the job because they are consciously seeking out improved class positions.

The gendered processes that can be found in hairdressing are similar to those that can be found in nursing, social work and exotic dancing. In particular, emotional competence, especially emotional caring, is valuable within this occupation. In addition, a high-fashion aesthetic is encouraged, commodified and capitalised on by workers within this industry, although this aesthetic is less sexualised and less overt than in the exotic dancing industry. These embodiments are often associated with femininity and so it appears that they operate as feminine capital in this occupation.

Vertical segregation exists within this occupation, just as it does in nursing and social work. Adam has experienced much greater advantage and success within the industry than the women. In addition, the hairdressers all testified that men dominate the upper echelons of hairdressing and it is mostly men who attain the celebrity positions. However, Adam's narrative suggested that it is most probably men who wield both masculinity *and* femininity that experience the most success. Moreover, this chapter does demonstrate how men in this occupation can step outside of normative gender boundaries. Adam's narrative shows how rules can be bent and gender re-imagined, even for working-class men. As Linsday comments:

> 'If gender is, as Connell argued, defined in relation to a particular job and the labour market as a whole, then working-class, heterosexual men working in the highly feminised hairdressing industry occupy an anomalous gender position (Connell 1995)'.
>
> (Lindsay, 2007: 273)

The next chapter, the final chapter of this book, discusses the commonalities and differences in the findings across the 'case study' chapters and draws some conclusions about the significance of a Bourdieusian approach and the concept of gender capital for understanding occupational gender segregation.

# 9
# Conclusions

Bourdieu (2001: 102) argued that the researcher must examine gender relations '*in the whole set of social spaces and subspaces*' including, occupational spaces, 'to explode the fantastical image of the "eternal feminine"'. This book has taken up Bourdieusian and feminist-Bourdieusian concepts in order to do just this, but also to examine how class is implicated in feminising processes. Making use of four 'case study' occupations, I have shown how there is both proximity and distance between feminised jobs and their participants and this is influenced by the capitals that are valued in these spaces and the statuses and capitals held by the workers they attract. In addition, occupations are implicated in the production and reproduction of workers' identities, capitals and practices. A number of findings were therefore consistent across the four occupations and so may be applicable to other forms of feminised work. In this last chapter I will discuss some of these consistencies that occurred in the workers' stories and the relevance of these findings for understanding emotional and aesthetic labour, gendered occupational segregation, gender capital and for 'using Bourdieu'.

## Understanding feminised occupational spaces

### Consistent choices

The findings certainly suggest that women's career choices do continue to be constrained by gender. Many of the female workers were following norms and family traditions or were completely unreflexive about their career choices so that their decisions to enter these jobs did not appear to be their own. Therefore, symbolic violence is often enacted in the occupational choice process. This means that gender continues to limits women's work practices in significant ways. In addition, the narratives also indicated that choices to work in these jobs seem to fall in line with class positions and dispositions as well so that classed habituses and class sanctions appear to direct many of the workers' actions.

## The structure of female and feminine capitals

However, this book has demonstrated that within feminised work gender is wielded as capital by men and women, sometimes quite consciously, and this does indicate that, although women may sometimes have few or no other assets available to them, some agency is involved in their participation in feminised work. In particular, feminised work appears to provide security or a path for mobility for working-class individuals. The men and many of the working-class women consciously sought out these jobs because they saw them as avenues for mobility. Hence, when other capitals are scarce, feminine capital in particular is an important asset for people from poorer socio-economic backgrounds. In this way gender cuts across class. In particular, because it is connected to women's bodies and is considered 'natural' for women, this gender capital is an asset that is more readily available to working-class women than other capitals might be. Perhaps, in this way, feminine capital is a democratised asset – it is available, in some form, to many women of all classes.

Moreover, this book has demonstrated that female and feminine capitals are similarly structured across the different occupations. For example, female nurses and social workers recognised that they are privileged in their occupations because a 'sisterhood' exists. In these circumstances feminine bodies and dispositions are not necessary – simply being hailed as female aids employment. The exotic dancers also asserted that almost any female body will enable entrance into their occupation. However, agents who embody a particular feminine aesthetic are more likely to be hired and once entrance to exotic dancing is achieved these bodies need to be worked on so that a sexualised hyper-femininity is produced. Similarly in hairdressing, a high-fashion feminine aesthetic is an asset and is cultivated by workers. Hence, in both hairdressing and exotic dancing particularly feminine female bodies are valuable and are therefore commodified and capitalised on. Moreover, nurses and social workers' female bodies are sometimes assets just because they are hailed as feminine (regardless of their identities or actions). Feminine bodies are capital in feminised work.

What is more, emotional competence and in particular, caring dispositions, are currency within all of these jobs and all of the groups of workers linked these competencies to femininity and so this makes these assets feminine capital. Nursing and social work are the two occupations that appear to most value emotional caring or 'caring about' and for this reason, among others, they may occupy the same field – the paid caring field. In addition, caring dispositions are useful and capitalised on in hairdressing and exotic dancing, although in exotic dancing, it is not caring alone that is important. Competency in 'hustling' or strategic flirting is most profitable in this occupation in interactions with customers. Hustling requires sophisticated communication skills and a kind of emotional intelligence in order to anticipate clients' desires and feelings.

### Class and feminine capital

Emotional competencies are perceived as feminine but they are also classed. In nursing and social work caring was more significant for the middle-class workers and it seems that a caring disposition is a particularly important aspect of middle-class femininity; 'caring about' is a feminine practice of distinction. This does not mean that the working-class women are not capable of caring (although Reay (2004) suggests that middle-class mothers are more likely to capitalise on emotions in the schooling system and Hochschild (1983) suggests that working-class and middle-class children are socialised to do emotions differently) but it may be that caring is less significant for working-class women's class identities and does not outweigh their need for economic capital. In addition, a middle- and upper-class feminine aesthetic is most valued in high-end hairdressing salons and strip clubs. In strip clubs the most profitable aesthetic is white, thin, tanned, blonde and often (but not always) big breasted. However, this does not mean that these dispositions and appearances cannot be performed or produced through work on the body. These attributes might be easier for better positioned women to attain but they are not out of the reach of poorer workers. Indeed, these performances are important for workers who have class aspirations as they give a sense of mobility, provide a sense of escape from the mundane through 'glamour' and (for exotic dancers) a sense of empowerment (which disproves some of Bourdieu's (1984) assertions about access to beauty capital). Furthermore, working-class dispositions are sometimes of some value as well. For example, Eliza suggested that the working class are more resilient and Ruth suggested something similar when she stated that her working-class background makes her a better social worker. Hence, as Skeggs (2004) suggests, it may be useful to rework the definition of capital so that it is not only associated with high culture practices.

### Performances and the impact of occupational spaces on dispositions

As this book has found that feminine competencies are adopted by men, middle-class femininity is adopted by working-class women and women do not always find that feminine competencies come to them easily, this book had demonstrated that femininity may sometimes be performed. This means that dispositions may be altered to fit with workplaces and that gendered embodiments might not be as fixed as Bourdieu suggested. In addition, while a 'fit' seems to have been developed between emotion and aesthetic work and women, this is not necessarily because women do it best, rather as Bourdieu and also Atkinson (2009) suggest, environments can impact dispositions; feminine workplaces produce feminine dispositions.

### Transgressing gender norms

While feminised spaces often serve to consolidate normative gender identities for women, the experiences of the nurses and hairdressers indicate that these occupational spaces open up possibilities for men to transgress gender norms. As Ahmed (2006), in his research on beauty work, and Hall, Hockney and Robinson (2007), in their study on hairdressing (as well as real estate agents and fire fighters) have found, feminised work contexts can produce a variety of masculinities. Again, feminised occupational contexts may impact dispositions, and a consequence of this is that they open up multiple ways for men to do gender. In addition, as McNay (2000) argues, these transgressions might be, in part, enabled by men's movement into and across fields (in this case occupational social spaces) – this type of movement can have a destabilising impact on gender identity. Or alternatively, these transgressions may be evidence that gender reflexivity is, as Adkins (2004: 202) suggests, a 'habit of gender' in the new economy. Further, the findings of this book suggest that men are willing to invest in, and openly utilise feminine dispositions and performances, when femininity is profitable. This indicates that if femininity held greater value it might be taken up more frequently by men.

### Limited capitals

However, this book has also shown that while female and feminine capitals are profitable in these occupations, it does seem that female and feminine capitals do come at a price. The women who invest themselves in caring and naturalise this disposition for women potentially cut themselves off from masculine arenas of social life. In addition, the women who invest in a sexualised hyper-feminine aesthetic achieve (temporal) glamour and economic capital but when it is used within the sex industry and without other middle-class indicators this is at the cost of depleted respectability and injured social relationships; their working-class positions and habituses impact the profit that they may gain from femininity. This means that feminine advantage does not override working-class disadvantage.

Furthermore, gender limits class advantage so that those women who come from middle-class backgrounds and occupy middle-class positions only experience limited advantage in middle-class occupational spaces. So, for example, nurses and social workers in management find that while their class backgrounds may provide them with a good 'feel for the game' this capital combined with their feminine and female capitals does not trump masculine and male capitals. So it seems, as Bourdieu (2001: 93) stated women are '*separated from men by a negative symbolic co-efficient*'. There is a 'diminution of symbolic capital entailed by being a woman' (Bourdieu, 2001: 93) and it seems that gender interacts with class in a way that nullifies its institutional backing and limits its strategic uses for women. Furthermore, as Skeggs (1997) has suggested, when gender capital is wielded by women, it is only a tactical rather than strategic asset – it may only manipulate constraints in the absence of power. Hence, when women move out of feminised work or compete with men, the symbolic value of their capital is not assured.

In addition, as this work is so closely associated with women and emotions and feminine aesthetics it does seem that men risk the experience of stigmatisation if they choose to participate in these occupations. Many of the men shared stories of symbolic violence. In particular, their masculinity and sexuality are questioned when they participate in this work, and this appears to impact their social status outside of these occupations. Men therefore pay for their contribution to feminised work in their personal relationships and in the 'economy of symbolic goods' (Bourdieu, 2001: 107). Perhaps, for this reason, the men I interviewed attempted to highlight their masculinity as well as femininity and depict their jobs as masculine.

Lastly, all of these occupations are attributed lower status than equivalent masculinised occupations, and so, of course, while gender capital helps to explain men's and women's attraction to feminised work as well as their successes and challenges within this work, the advantages that feminine capital can provide to both men and women is limited.

For this reason, workers struggled over the meanings of their occupations and frequently attempted to make them more valuable within their narratives, and for this reason many women still experience limited options in the labour market.

## Understanding emotional and aesthetic labour

As the discussion above indicates, my findings also build on previous understandings of emotional and aesthetic labour in interactive body work. Other writers (see McDowell, 2009) have talked about how employers in the service industry look for certain dispositions in employees and how these dispositions are then worked upon and commodified. This book has looked at this phenomenon from another angle, and has argued for the existence of a gender economy where not only employers but *employees* capitalise on gender embodiments. While previous research has found that this work is gendered (for example see Black, 2004; Hochschild, 1983; McDowell, 2009) and classed (Hochschild, 1983), this book has argued that emotional competence and certain bodily aesthetics operate as *capital* in the labour market. More specifically they are feminine capitals because they are aligned with femininity and so are seen to be possessed by women, are often wielded by women and are valued in feminised work. In addition, while some commentators argue that emotional labour is harmful for workers (for example, Hochschild (1983) argues that it produces alienation in workers), the findings presented in this book suggest that although emotional labour can produce stress, 'doing gender well' also enables mobility, consolidates class identity and position, may even be desired (as was the case for many nurses and social workers) and may bring pleasure (particularly for hairdressers).

## Bourdieu and gender segregation

Gendered occupational segregation is persistent and widespread yet inadequately understood. I hope that this book has demonstrated that a Bourdieusian approach, with a focus on 'experience, dispositions, struggles and social difference and distance' (Atkinson, 2009; 909), can contribute to a better understanding of the processes that perpetuate gender divisions in the labour force. However, I have also argued with feminists (including Moi (1991), Skeggs (1997), Lovell (2000) McNay (1999), Reay (2004) and Silva (2005)) that it is also necessary to move beyond Bourdieu in order to allow for a thorough analysis of agency, performance and the transgression of gender norms and to understand gender as centrally located in social space. In particular, the feminist-Bourdieusian concept 'gender capital' highlights the significance of a gender economy for organising gender relations. I have shown that 'gender capital' is a concept that helps to explain why women are still invested in, and contribute to, the making of feminised occupations and helps to explain why men continue to retain distance from this work but also experience such success when they do participate. Importantly, this concept helps to demonstrate that women do not necessarily do feminine work because they are feminine and men are not incapable of embodying and performing femininity. This means that horizontal gendered occupational segregation is not inevitable. Moreover, I hope that I have demonstrated that the concept 'gender capital' helps to explain the role of class in feminising processes. Gender capital is a unique concept in that it assists in unravelling a relationship that is complex and like all social intersections, difficult to understand: the relationship between gender, class and occupation.

# Notes

## 2 Why Use Bourdieusian Theory to Study Gender, Class and Work? The Case for 'Gender Capital'

1. Kath and Kim are from the Australian television comedy 'Kath and Kim' and Vicky Pollard is from the British television comedy 'Little Britain'.

## 3 Gender and Class in Four Occupations

1. In the UK there are state-enrolled nurses (SENs), however training for enrolled nursing no longer exists, although there is an 'Access to Higher Education Diploma in Nursing' available from further education colleges that provides an alternative route to the university degree or higher education diploma. In addition diplomas will no longer exist in the UK after 2013 – only a nursing degree will be offered. There are, however, senior health care assistants or senior nursing auxiliaries who assist registered nurses but are not authorised to administer medication. Health care assistants and nursing auxiliaries often qualify through the apprenticeship system or via the Open University.

# References

ACOSS (Australian Council of Social Services) (2003) *Barriers to University Participation: ACOSS Submission to the Senate Inquiry into Higher Education*, October, 2003, Australian Council for Social Services: Redfern.

Adkins, L. (2004) 'Reflexivity: Freedom of Habit or Gender?' in L. Adkins and B. Skeggs (Eds) *Feminism after Bourdieu*, Oxford: Blackwell Publishing/The Sociological Review.

Adkins, L. (2005) 'The New Economy, Property and Personhood', *Theory Culture and Society*, vol. 22, pp. 111–30.

Adkins, L. and Lury, C. (1999) 'The Labour of Identity: performing identities, performing economies', *Economy and Society*, pp. 598–614.

Ahmed, S. (2006) 'Making Beautiful: male workers in beauty parlors', *Men and Masculinities*, vol. 9, pp. 168–85.

Alvesson, M. (1998) 'Gender Relations and Identity at Work: A Case Study of Masculinities and Femininities in an Advertising Agency', *Human Relations*, vol. 51, no. 8, pp. 969–1005.

Anonymous (2007) 'Nurses' Wages Still Lower than UK Average', *Nursing Standard* vol. 22, no. 14–16, pp. 9–9.

Atkinson, W. (2009) 'Rethinking the Work-Class Nexus: Theoretical Foundations for Recent Trends', *Sociology*, vol. 43, no. 5, pp. 896–912.

Attwood, M. and Hatton, F. (1983) 'Getting On. Gender Differences in Career Development' in Eva Gamarnikow, David Morgan, June Purvis and Daphne Taylorson (Eds) *Gender, Class and Work*, Heinemann: London.

Australian Bureau of Statistics (ABS) (2005a) *Australian Social Trends: Income Distribution*, http://www.abs.gov.au/Ausstats/abs@.nsf/0/BAC94EBF241B1C9C CA25703B0080CCC8?opendocument, date accessed 31 January 2012.

Australian Bureau of Statistics (ABS) (2005b) *Australian Social Trends: Work: Nursing Workers*, www.abs.gov.au/ausstats, date accessed 22 January 2006.

Australian Bureau of Statistics (ABS) (2011) *Gender Indicators: Labour Force*, July 2011, http://www.abs.gov.au/ausstats/abs@.nsf/Lookup/by+Subject/ 4125.0~Jul+2011~Main+Features~Labour+force~1110, date accessed 26 March 2011.

Australian Council of Trade Unions (ACTU) (2004) *Fact Sheet: Casual and Insecure Employment in Australia*, www.actu.asn.au/public/news, date accessed 16 March 2006.

Australian Institute of Health and Welfare (AIHW) (2010) Nursing and midwifery labour force 2008, http://www.aihw.gov.au/labourforce/nurses.cfm, date accessed 31 January 2011.

Australian Nursing Federation (ANF) (2011) *Fact Sheet 2: A Snapshot of Nursing in Australia*, http://www.anf.org.au/pdf/Fact_Sheet_Snap_Shot_Nursing.pdf, date accessed 12 March 2012.

Barber, K. (2008) 'The Well-Coiffed Man: Class, Race and Heterosexual Masculinity in the Hair Salon', *Gender and Society*, vol. 22, no. 4, pp. 455–76.

Bauman, Z. (2005) *Work, Consumerism and the New Poor*, Maidenhead: Open University Press.

Beck, U. (2007) 'Beyond Class and Nation: reframing social inequalities in a globalized world', *The British Journal of Sociology*, vol. 58, no. 4, pp. 679–705.

Benson, R. and Neveu, E. (2005) *Bourdieu and the Journalistic Field*. Cambridge: Polity.

Bindel, J. (2004) *Profitable Exploits: Lap Dancing in the UK*, Child and Woman Abuse Studies Unit, London Metropolitan University and Glasgow City Council.

Black, P. (2004) *The Beauty Industry: Gender, Culture, Pleasure*, London: Routledge.

Bourdieu, P. (1984) *Distinction: A Social Critique of the Judgment of Taste*, London: Routledge (translated by Richard Nice).

Bourdieu, P. (1986) 'The Forms of Capital'. in J. E. Richardson (Ed.) *Handbook of a Theory of Research for the Sociology of Education*, New York: Greenwood Press, Translated by Richard Nice, pp. 241–58.

Bourdieu, P. (1990) 'La Domination Masculine', *Actes de la recherche en sciences Sociales*, vol. 84, pp. 2–31.

Bourdieu, P. (1990a) *Outline of a Theory of Practice*. Cambridge: Cambridge University Press.

Bourdieu, P. (2001) *Masculine Domination*, Cambridge: Polity Press (translated by Richard Nice).

Bourdieu, P. and Boltanski, L. (1981) 'The Educational System and the Economy: Titles and Jobs', in C. C. Lemert (Ed.) *French Sociology: Rupture and Renewal Since 1968*, New York: Columbia University Press, pp. 141–51.

Bourdieu, P. and Wacquant, L. (1992) *An Invitation to Reflexive Sociology*, Cambridge: Polity Press.

Bott, E. (2006) 'Pole Position: Migrant British Women Producing "Selves" Through Lap Dancing Work' *Feminist Review*, no. 83, pp. 23–41.

Brooks, S. (2010) *Unequal Desires: Race and Erotic Capital in the Stripping Industry*, New York: SUNY Press.

Brown, S. (1986) 'A Woman's Profession', in H. Marchant and B. Marchant (Eds) *Gender Reclaimed: Women in Social Work*, Hale and Iremonger: Sydney.

Brown, C. and Jones, L. (2004) 'The Gender Structure of the Nursing Hierarchy: The Role of Human Capital', *Gender, Work and Organization*, vol. 11, no. 1, January 2004, pp. 1–25.

Butler, J. (1997) *Excitable Speech*, NewYork: Routledge.

Chase, S. (2003) 'Taking Narrative Seriously: Consequences for Method and Theory in Interview Studies', in Y. Lincoln and N. Denzin (Eds) (2003) *Turning Points in Qualitative Research: Tying Knots in Handkerchiefs*, Walnut: Altamira Press/Rowman & Littlefield Publishers.

Christie, A. (1998) 'Is Social Work a Non-Traditional Occupation for Men?' *British Journal of Social Work*, vol. 28, pp. 491–510.

Connell, R. W. (1991) 'Live Fast and Die Young: The Construction of Masculinity among Young Working-class Men on the Margins of the Labour Market', *Journal of Sociology*, vol. 27, pp. 141–71.

Coy, M. and Garner, M. (2010) 'Glamour Modelling and the Marketing of Self-Sexualization: Critical Reflection', *International Journal of Cultural Studies*, vol. 13, pp. 657–75.

Department of Education, Employment and Workplace Relations (DEEWR) (2009) *A Skills Gap Analaysis of Hairdressing in Australia – an Occupation in Demand or a Demanding Occupation?* August 2009.

Deshotels, T. and Forsyth, C. (2006) 'Strategic Flirting and the Emotional Tab of Exotic Dancing' *Deviant Behavior*, vol. 27, no. 2, pp. 223–41.

Dyer, S., McDowell, L. and Batnitzky, A. (2008) 'Emotional Labour/Body Work: The Caring Labours of Migrants in the UK's National Health Service', *Geoforum*, vol. 39, pp. 2030–8.

de Certeau, M. (1988) 'The Practice of Everyday Life'. London: University of California Press.

Evans, J. (2004) 'Men Nurses: A Historical and Feminist Perspective', *Journal of Advanced Nursing*, vol. 47, no. 3, pp. 321–8.

Fowler, B. (2003) 'Reading Pierre Bourdieu's *Masculine Domination*: Notes Towards an Intersectional Analysis of Gender, Culture and Class', *Cultural Studies*, vol. 13, no. 3–4, pp. 468–94.

Frank, K. (2007) 'Thinking Critically about Strip Club Research', *Sexualities*, vol. 10 no. 4, pp. 501–17.

Furlong, A. and Kelly, P. (2005) 'The Brazilianisation of Youth Transitions in Australia and the UK?' *Australian Journal of Social Issues*, Summer, vol. 40, no. 4, pp. 207–26.

Gall, G. (2007) 'Sex Work Unionisation: an Exploratory Study of Emerging Collective Organisation', *Industrial Relations Journal*, vol. 38, no. 1, pp. 70–88.

Gamarnikow, E. (1978) 'Sexual Division of Labour: The Case of Nursing', in A. Kuhn and A. M. Wolfe (Eds) *Feminism and Materialism*, London: Routledge and Kegan Paul.

Game, A. and Pringle, R. (1983) *Gender at Work*, Chapter Five, North Sydney: Allen and Unwin, pp. 94–118.

Gimlin, D. (1996) 'Pamela's Place: Power and Negotiation in the Hair Salon', *Gender & Society*, vol. 10, no. 5, pp. 505–26.

Glover, D. and Radcliffe, M. (1998) 'Why is Success in Nursing a Boy Thing?' *Nursing Times*, August 12, vol. 94, no. 32, p. 13.

Habia (2008) *Industry Statistics*, November 2008, http://www.habia.org/uploads/ Habia%20Stats%20November%202008.pdf, date accessed 28 March 2012.

Hall, A., Hockney, J. and Robinson, V. (2007) 'Occupational Cultures and the Embodiment of Masculinity: Hairdressing, Estate Agency and Firefighting', *Gender, Work and Organization*, vol. 14, no. 6, pp. 534–51.

Harker, R., Mahar, C. and Wilkes, C. (Eds) (1990) *An Introduction to the Work of Bourdieu: The Practice of Theory*, London: Palgrave Macmillan.

Hochschild, A. (1983) *A Managed Heart: Commercialization of Human Feeling*, University of California Press: Berkeley.

Honneth, A. (2000) 'The Fragmented World of Symbolic Forms: Reflections on Pierre Bourdieu's Sociology of Culture' in D. Robbins (Ed.) *Pierre Bourdieu*, Sage Publication: London, vol. 3.

Howe, D. (1985) 'The Segregation of Women and their Work in the Personal Social Services', *Critical Social Policy*, vol. 5, no. 21, pp. 21–35.

Hubbard, P. (2008) *Encouraging Sexual Exploitation? Regulating Striptease and 'Adult Entertainment' in the UK*, Loughborough's Institutional Repository.

Huppatz, K. (2009) 'Reworking Bourdieu's "Capital": Feminine and Female Capitals in the Field of Paid Caring Work' *Sociology*, vol. 43, no. 1, pp. 45–66.

Huppatz, K. (2010) 'Class and Career Choice: Motivations, Aspirations, Identity and Mobility for Women in Paid Caring Work', *Health Sociology Review*, no. 46, pp. 115–32.

Illouz, E. (1997) 'Who Will Take Care of the Caretakers Daughter? Towards a Sociology of Happiness in the Era of Reflexive Modernity', *Theory, Culture and Society*, vol. 14, no. 4, pp. 31–66.

Krais, B. (2006) 'Gender, Sociological Theory and Bourdieu's Sociology of Practice', *Theory, Culture and Society*, vol. 23, no. 6, pp. 119–34.

Langellier, K. (2003) 'Personal Narrative, Performance, Performativity: Two or Three Things I Know for Sure', in Y. Lincoln and D. Norman (Eds) (2003) *Turning Points in Qualitative Research: Tying Knots in Handkerchiefs*, Walnut: Altamira Press/Rowman & Littlefield Publishers.

Lawler, S. (1999) 'Getting Out and Getting Away': Women's Narratives of Class Mobility', *Feminist Review*, no. 23, Autumn, pp. 3–24.

Levy, A (2005) *Female Chauvinist Pigs: Women and the Rise of Raunch Culture*, Collingwood: Black Inc.

Lewis, I. (2004) 'Gender and Professional Identity: A Qualitative Study of Social Workers Practicing as Counsellors and Psychotherapists', *Australian Social Work*, December 2004, vol. 57, no. 4, pp. 394–407.

Lincoln, Y. and Denzin, N. (2003) 'The Methodological Revolution' in Yvonna Lincoln and Norman Denzin (Eds) (2003) *Turning Points in Qualitative Research: Tying Knots in Handkerchiefs*, Walnut Creek: Altamira Press/Rowman & Littlefield Publishers.

Lindsay, J. (2004) 'Gender and Class in the Lives of Young Hairdressers: From Serious to Spectacular', *Journal of Youth Studies*, vol. 7, no. 3, September, pp. 259–77.

Lovell, T. (2000) 'Thinking Feminism With and Against Bourdieu', *Feminist Theory*, vol. 1, no. 1, pp. 11–32.

Marsland, L., Robinson, S. and Murrels, T. (1996) 'Pursuing a Career in Nursing: Differences Between Men and Women Qualifying as Registered General Nurses', *Journal of Nursing Management*, vol. 4, pp. 231–41.

Martin, E. (1996) 'An Update on Census Data: Good News for Social Work?' *Australian Social Work*, June, vol. 49, no. 2, pp. 29–36.

Mavin, S. and Gandy, G. (2011) 'Doing Gender Well and Differently in Dirty Work: The Case of Exotic Dancing', *Gender, Work and Organization*, 4 August 2011.

McCall, L. (1992) 'Does Gender *Fit*? Bourdieu, Feminism, and the Concepts of Social Order', *Theory and Society*, vol. 21, pp. 837–67.

McDowell, L. (1997) *Capital Culture: Gender at Work in the City*, Oxford: Blackwell Publishers.

McDowell, L. (2000) 'The Trouble with Men? Young People, Gender Transformations and the Crisis of Masculinity', *International Journal of Urban and Regional Research*, vol. 24, no. 1, pp. 201–9.

McDowell, L. (2008) 'Thinking through Class and Gender in the Context of Working Class Studies', *Antipode*, pp. 20–4.

McDowell, L. (2009) *Working Bodies: Interactive Service Employment and Workplace Identities*, West Sussex: Wiley-Blackwell.

McKenna, L., Sadler, R., Long, M. and Burke, G. (2001) *National Review of Nursing Education: Enrolled Nursing Education*, Canberra: Commonwealth Department of Education, Science and Training.

McNay, L. (1999) 'Gender, Habitus and the Field: Pierre Bourdieu and the Limits of Reflexivity', *Theory, Culture and Society*, vol. 16, no. 1, pp. 95–117.

McNay, L. (2000) *Gender and Agency: Reconfiguring the Subject in Feminist and Social Theory*, Cambridge: Polity Press.

McNay, L. (2004) *Agency and Experience: Gender as a Lived Relation*, in L. Adkins and B. Skeggs (Eds) *Feminism After Bourdieu*, Oxford: Blackwell Publishing/The Sociological Review, pp. 175–90.

Meagher, G. and Healy, K. (2005) *Who Cares? Volume 1: A Profile of Care Workers in Australia's Community Services Industries*, Paper 140, June 2005, Strawberry Hills: Australian Council for Social Services.

Mercer, M., Buchan, J. and Chubb, C. (2010) 'Flexible Nursing: Report for NHS Professionals, Institute for Employment Studies', Brighton, http://www.employment-studies.co.uk/pdflibrary/184nhsp.pdf, date accessed 31 January 2011.

Mendes, P. (2005) 'The History of Social Work in Australia: A Critical Literature Review' *Australian Social Work*, vol. 58, no. 2, pp. 121–31.

Miers, M. (2000) *Gender Issues and Nursing Practice*, Hampshire: Macmillan Press.

Moi, T. (1991) 'Appropriating Bourdieu: Feminist Theory and Pierre Bourdieu's Sociology of Culture', *New Literary History*, vol. 22, no. 4, pp. 1017–49.

Murdock, G. (2000) 'Class Stratification and Cultural Consumption: Some Motifs in the Work of Pierre Bourdieu (1977)' in D. Robbins (Ed.) *Pierre Bourdieu*, London: Sage Publication.

Nelson, S. (2001) 'Hairdressing and Nursing: Presentation of the Self and Professional Formation in Colonial Australia', *Collegian*, vol. 8, no. 2, pp. 28–31.

Perry, R. and Cree, V. (2003) 'The Changing Gender Profile of Applicants to Qualifying Social Work Training in the UK', *Social Work Education*, vol. 22, no. 4, 375–83.

Pettinger, L. (2005) 'Gendered Work Meets Gendered Goods: Selling and Service in Clothing Retail', *Gender, Work and Organization*, vol. 12, no. 5, pp. 460–79.

Powell, G. and Graves, L. (2003) *Women and Men in Management*, California: Sage.

Price-Glynn, K. (2010) *Strip Club: Gender, Power and Sex Work*, New York: New York University Press.

Pudney, S. and Shields, M. (2000) 'Gender and Racial Discrimination in Pay and Promotion for NHS Nurses', *Oxford Bulletin of Economics and Statistics* vol. 62, pp. 801–35.

Reay, D. (1997) 'Feminist Theory, Habitus, and Social Class: Disrupting Notions of Classlessness' *Women's Studies International Forum*, vol. 20, no. 2, pp. 225–33.

Reay, D. (2004) 'Gendering Bourdieu's Concept of Capitals? Emotional Capital, Women and Social Class', in L. Adkins and B. Skeggs (Eds) *Feminism after Bourdieu*, Oxford: Blackwell, pp. 57–74.

Robinson, V., Hall, A. and Hockey, J. (2011) 'Masculinities, Sexualities and the Limits of Subversion: Being a Man in Hairdressing', *Men and Masculinities*, vol. 14, no. 1, pp. 31–50.

Saffron, A. (2008) 'Life as the Son of Gentle Satan', *The Canberra Times*, http://www.canberratimes.com.au/news/local/news/news-features/life-as-the-son-of-gentle-satan/1227599.aspx?storypage=0, date accessed 10 February 2012.

Sharma, U. and Black, P. (2001) 'Look Good, Feel Better: Beauty Therapy as Emotional Labour', *Sociology*, vol. 35, no. 4, pp. 913–31.

Shepherd, J. (2009) 'White, Middle Class Families Dominate Top University Places', *The Guardian*, Tuesday 3 February 2009, http://www.guardian.co.uk/education/2009/feb/03/universities-admissions-social-mobility, date accessed 15 September 2011.

Shilling, C. (1991) 'Educating the Body: Physical Capital and the Production of Social Inequalities', *Sociology* vol. 25, no. 4, pp. 653–72.

Shteir, R. (2004) 'Striptease: the untold history of the girlie show', New York: Oxford University Press.

Silva, E. (2005) 'Gender, Home and Family in Cultural Capital Theory', *The British Journal of Sociology*, vol. 56, no. 1, pp. 83–103.

Skeggs, B. (1997) *Formations of Class and Gender: Becoming Respectable*. London: Sage.

Skeggs, B. (2004) 'Context and Background: Pierre Bourdieu's Analysis of Class, Gender and Sexuality', in L. Adkins and B. Skeggs (Eds) *Feminism after Bourdieu*, Oxford: Blackwell Publishing, pp. 19–34.

Shulman, C. (2011) 'Tough Times: the Industry Faces Increased Competition from Matchmaking Sites' *IBISWorld Industry Report Q9528: Sexual Services in Australia*, November 2011.

Smith, C. (2002) 'Shiny Chests and Heaving G Strings: A Night Out With the Chippendales' *Sexualities*, vol. 5, no. 67, pp. 67–89.

Stewart, H. (2011) 'Working for nothing – the truth about low pay in the UK' *The Observer*, Sunday 2 October 2011, Retrieved from: http://www.guardian.co.uk/society/2011/oct/02/low-pay-uk-living-wage, 28 March 2012.

Strip Clubs Australia (2011) www.stripclubsaustralia.net, date accessed January 11, 2012.

TAFESA (2006) *Counsellor/Community Worker*, www.vlepubsa.edu.au/xml/profiles, date accessed 19 Januray 2006.

The Trade and Industry Committee (2005) *Jobs for the Girls: the Effect of Occupational Segregation on the Gender Pay Gap*, Sixteenth Report of Session 2004–5, House of Commons, 22 March 2005, http://www.publications.parliament.uk/pa/cm200405/cmselect/cmtrdind/300/300.pdf, date accessed 27 March 2012.

Trautner, M. (2005) 'Doing Gender, Doing Class: the Performance of Sexuality in Exotic Dancing Clubs' *Gender and Society*, vol. 19, no. 6, pp. 771–88.

Tyler, M., Jeffreys, S., Rave, N., Norma, C., Quek, Main, A. and Chambers, K. (2010) *Not Just Harmless Fun: The Strip Industry in Victoria*, Coalition Against Trafficking Women.

Ungerson, C. (1983) 'Why Do Women Care?', in J. Finch and D. Groves (Eds) *A Labour of Love: Women, Work and Caring*, London: Routledge and Kegan Paul pp. 31–50.

Walby, S. and Olsen, W. (2002) *The Impact of Women's Position in the Labour Market on Pay and Implication for UK Productivity, Women and Equality Unit*, November 2002.

Walton, R. (1975) *Women in Social Work*, London: Routledge and Kegan Paul.

Weininger, E. (2005) 'Foundations of Pierre Bourdieu's Class Analysis', in E. O. Wright (Ed.) *Approaches to Class Analysis*, Cambridge: Cambridge University Press.

West, C. and Zimmerman, D. (1987) 'Doing Gender', *Gender and Sexuality*, vol. 1, no. 2, pp. 125–51.

Williams, L. and Connell, C. (2010) 'Employee Experience of Aesthetic Labour in Retail and Hospitality', *Work Employment & Society*, vol. 21, no. 1, pp. 103–20.

Witz, A. (1992) *Professions and Patriarchy*, Routledge: London.

Witz, A., Warhurst, C. and Nickson, D. (2003) 'The Labour of Aesthetics and the Aesthetics of Organization' *Organization*, vol. 10, no. 1, pp. 33–54.

Wright, C. M., Frew, T. J. and Hatcher, D. (1998) 'Social and Demographic Characteristics of Young and Mature Aged Nursing Students in Australian Universities', *Nurse Education Today*, vol. 18, no. 2, pp. 101–7.

Wolf, V. (1927) *To the Lighthouse*, New York: Harvest Books.

# Index